THE FLOWERING OF
MUSLIM THEOLOGY

THE FLOWERING OF

MUSLIM THEOLOGY

Josef van Ess

Translated by Jane Marie Todd

HARVARD UNIVERSITY PRESS
Cambridge, Massachusetts, and London, England
2006

Originally published as *Prémices de la théologie musulmane,*
© Éditions Albin Michel S.A., 2002

This book was published with the support of the
French Ministry of Culture—National Book Center /
Cet ouvrage a été publié avec l'assistance du Ministère
chargé de la culture—Centre National du Livre.

Library of Congress Cataloging-in-Publication Data

Ess, Josef van.
[Prémices de la théologie musulmane. English]
The flowering of Muslim theology / Josef van Ess;
translated by Jane Marie Todd.
p. cm.
"This book began as a series of four lectures given by Josef van Ess
at the Institut du monde arabe, Paris, in 1998."
Includes bibliographical references and index.
ISBN 0-674-02208-4
1. Islam—Theology.   2. Islam—Doctrines.   I. Title.
BP166.E7713 2006
299.2—dc22   2005052792

CONTENTS

NOTE TO THE ENGLISH-LANGUAGE EDITION

THIS BOOK BEGAN as a series of four lectures given by Josef van Ess at the Institut du monde arabe, Paris, in 1998. These lectures constitute the first four chapters; the author added a fifth chapter and an introduction for publication as the book *Prémices de la théologie musulmane* (2002). In a way, this book is an introduction in French to van Ess's masterwork, *Theologie und Gesellschaft im 2. und 3. Jahrhundert Hidschra* (Theology and society in the second and third centuries AH).

THE FLOWERING OF
MUSLIM THEOLOGY

INTRODUCTION

IN THE MASS MEDIA, Islam is the "Other," repellent and strange. The notion commonly associated with it is the Sharia, Islamic law based on the Koran, which would seem to be incompatible with the rules of enlightened reason. That view contrasts sharply with what Tāhā Husayn wrote in *The Future of Culture in Egypt* (1938): "Everything seems to indicate that there is nothing to distinguish a European mind from the Eastern mind."[1] And he added: "I am certain that there is no difference in essence or in nature between us and the Europeans."[2] Mustafā 'Abd al-Rāziq repeated that idea in 1945, in the official speech he gave to inaugurate his new duties as sheikh al-Azhar, that is, as the head of a university that virtually embodies the spirit of the Sharia: "I see no real reason to set Islam and the West in opposition to each other."[3] At the time, these two Egyptian intellectuals could count on the assent of some Europeans. Johann Wolfgang von Goethe had declared: "Orient und

Okzident sind nicht mehr zu trennen" (East and West can no longer be separated). Like later Romantic writers, though, Goethe was thinking about poetry, especially Iranian poetry; by contrast, Tāhā Husayn and Mustafā 'Abd al-Rāziq were thinking of medieval philosophy and what emerged from it. In the Germany of the Romantics, Ibn Rushd (Averroës) had been lauded as the representative of Islamic enlightenment and considered a "rationalist" who had transmitted the legacy of enlightened Islam to a Europe still in limbo.[4] The film *Destiny,* by the Egyptian filmmaker Youssef Chahine, also disseminates that image. For Chahine, however, Islam has two faces, a notion that has become quite familiar to us.

It is not enough to speak of philosophy, or merely of fundamentalism and the law. A place must also be assigned to theology, *'ilm al-kalām,* as it was called, the "science of dialectical speech" practiced by those who knew how to "hold conversations" about their religion with those defending other interpretations, even if their interlocutors were not Muslim.[5] The word suggests that the "dialecticians" were engaged in apologetics. That is only partly true, however; theology would soon make other claims. The role it envisaged for itself was to provide an authentic explanation of the world. Hence it was naturally taken to be a "philosophy" at a time when the true *falsafa*, that of al-Kindī and his circle, of al-Fārābī and others, on up to Ibn Rushd—the only one that deserves to be called a philosophy in our modern view—had not yet made its appearance.

At that time, as in the eighteenth century in France, "philosophers" were simply intellectuals, and among them a group of *mutakallimūn* (those who practiced *kalām*) had the very highest status, alongside physicians and "men of science"–that is, astrologers and alchemists.[6] In his *Ketābā de sīmāta* (Book of treasures), Job of Edessa complained about the "new philosophers" who were gravitating around al-Nazzām, "vainly seeking the glory of the world."[7] For Job of Edessa, a Christian physician and defender of the Greek legacy, such men were mere grandstanders, undeserving of the reputation they enjoyed. For Muslims, however, they performed a function similar to that of the Church Fathers. They were not as immersed in the ideas of Plato and Aristotle as their Christian counterparts, but they had the same advantage Origen and Clement of Alexandria had had some centuries earlier: they still had historical options available to them, options that would become more limited later on. As a result, they enjoyed a freedom of thought that later generations could only dream of. For that reason, the *kalām* phenomenon reached its zenith very early; its most creative period did not occur after it had come of age, but well before, at a time when signs of tedium and paralysis had not yet appeared.

That fascinating world has now collapsed, submerged by the waves of puritanism that prefigured modern fundamentalism. In Saudi Arabia, *kalām* is excluded from the university curriculum—as is philosophy. We must not forget, however, that theology in the sense described here has always been confined to certain regions and certain moments in history, particularly Iraq during the early centuries of the Abbasid dynasty, and then Iran, where it flourished again until the Mongol empire. We are interested here in the beginnings, the time of open options when *kalām* was still deeply rooted in Muslim society. It held a rank equivalent to that of jurisprudence. The first Iraqi jurist, Abū Hanīfa, who made a lasting mark on Islamic law, left behind only his theological treatises (*Letter to ʿUthmān al-Battī* and the dialogues collected by his students, *Fiqh al-absat* and *Kitāb al-ʿālim waʾl-mutaʿallim*). His legal teachings seem to have been transmitted only through the oral tradition. The two disciplines were still rivals, and it was not at all obvious that jurisprudence would prevail.

Both benefited from their close relationship to their environment. Theologians were not concerned only with God and eternal truths; far from it. They also dealt with believers' everyday problems and personal worries. The theologians would begin to lose ground only after they grew hungry for power and allied themselves with the Abbasid court. The shock produced by the *mihna,* the inquisition launched under al-Ma'mūn, was immeasurable. Those accused of being the instigators—namely, the Mu'tazilite theologians—were not directly responsible for it. The initiative for that inquisition had been taken, rather, by the caliph. But the persecution campaign cost the Mu'tazilites the sympathy of all its victims, members both of the lower classes and of the middle class.

Before religious thinkers congregated in the capital, local orthodoxies of a sort had been created in cities such as al-Kufa, Basra, and Damascus, and they varied according to which option was chosen. This state of affairs is especially noteworthy when it comes to political theories; the positions differed from one city to the next. At a particular time, the following ideologies were "true" wherever they had arisen: Qadarism, Murji'ism, and the different forms of Shiism. Later, however, they were all considered heresies. Such was the influence exerted by the capital. In

Baghdad, the imported "orthodoxies" were amalgamated and underwent a process of attrition. The court acted as a catalyst; scholars in the "provinces" who wanted to pursue a career in the capital were forced to abandon local particularities or to refrain from openly propagating them. The geographer Ibn al-Faqīh wrote, "The good thing about Baghdad is that the government does not have to fear that one school will prevail over another as has happened in al-Kufa. There, the ʿAlids, alongside the Shiites, often manage to rule the population. In Baghdad, all of them—Shiites, Muʿtazilites, and Khārijites—coexist; each camp holds the others in check and prevents it from asserting its dominance."[8] Muʿtazilism, though originally an import from the city of Basra, was able to take advantage of the situation, creating the first orthodoxy in the Muslim world that extended beyond one locality. In broadening its theoretical base and establishing a new balance between the various views, it managed to avoid becoming diluted. The rationalism in which it took such pride was its most effective tool.

The aim of this book is to clarify a few aspects of that development. Its subject is historical, nothing more. Nevertheless, the Muslim worldview has conserved many traces of it. Muʿtazilism was replaced by

other orthodoxies, but the ideas it developed had a
subversive influence on later movements. Although
it was threatened in Baghdad in the late third century AH (ninth century CE), it managed to prevail in
Khwārazm in about AH 400 (1010 CE), thanks to its
missionary efforts. In AH 803 (1400–1401 CE), during
the Syrian campaign of Timur Lenk (Tamerlane), the
world conqueror was accompanied by a Hanafite jurist who was a Muʿtazilite. Ibn Khaldūn met him in
Damascus during the famous audience that Timur
Lenk granted him. In the end, Muʿtazilite orthodoxy
also became a local orthodoxy. Theological problems
may be eternal, but they are not static. The responses
that befit a given situation at a given time quickly
become rigid stereotypes. But sometimes they also
prove to be viable alternatives to those offered in our
own time. Therein lies their importance, for Muslims
and for us as well. Modern thought is heir to a rich
past, and recalling views and decisions that were once
taken seriously will always prove useful.

1

THEOLOGY IN ITS OWN EYES

Division and Heresy in Islam

HERESY OCCUPIES as vast a field in Islam as in Christianity. Is it really legitimate to confine it to the classical age? During the *mihna,* or inquisition, the marriage of Ibn Mālaj, a traditionalist who rejected the idea of the created Koran *(khalq al-Qur'ān),* was voided by the courts.[1] There is a striking parallel between that action and the present-day case of Nasr Abu Zayd in Egypt, despite the twelve centuries that separate them. In our own time, the Egyptian Islamist group Jamā'at al-Takfīr wa'l-Hijra inspires fear; but even in the ninth century CE, the Mu'tazilites had earned a reputation for their use of the *takfīr,* that is, for the anathematizing of their adversaries. Abū Hayyān al-Tawhīdī deplored the practice. Abū Hāshim, he said, had called his own father, al-Jubbā'ī, an infidel, and vice versa; Abū Hāshim's sister, he continued, had anathematized both her father and her brother. She was an emancipated woman; she headed a women's organization of sorts, whose aim seems to have been Mu'tazilite evangelization. As we know, the Mu'tazilites not only quarreled among themselves, but also directed considerable aggression toward the "others," the *hashwiyya,* the uneducated, the rabble. Is that because for at least a century the Mu'tazilites had been the elite, the intellectual "orthodoxy" of their time? The majority of theologians were still Mu'tazilites when al-Tawhīdī was writing. He concluded with a somewhat critical remark: "I do not really understand what *takfir* means for them! Why can't we put an end to that ordeal [*fitna*]?"[2]

Which of the two positions corresponded to the typical attitude of Muslim society during the classical period—the *takfir* practiced by certain intellectuals or al-Tawhīdī's discomfort with that behavior? I do not know whether I shall answer that question satisfactorily. But let me briefly consider the term used at the time, *kufr,* or unbelief. Christians would have preferred "heresy," and today we speak of tolerance and intolerance. My treatment will pay particular attention to word choice. There are always realities behind language, however—the context, the social structures or institutions (if they exist), and the founding doctrines: in this case, scripture, the Prophetic tradition, and historical myths.

The word for heresy in the European languages comes from the Greek. But in antiquity, *hairesis* meant simply "choice"; the word had no negative connotations. Any school of philosophy could be called a *hairesis,* and it was not considered scandalous or blameworthy to prefer one *hairesis* to another. It was only the Church Fathers who used the word to mean a reprehensible or foolish choice, a bad impulse—a *hawā,* as the Arabs and the Koran would later say. In the religions of antiquity no mention was made as yet of aberration or schism. Rather than reject a foreign faith, they incorporated and transformed its elements, a process known as syncretism. The only exception was Judaism, which introduced a new factor, revelation. At the time, Jewish theologians were wont to speak of their covenant with God. But the Israelites were not alone in doing so. The Christians understood the birth of their religion as a "new covenant," and the Muslims too possessed their *'ahd* or *mīthāq,* with a new book and new commandments. The words "pact" and "covenant" are legal notions; they imply the existence of an obligation, a *taklīf.* Heresy or aberration can therefore become

11

apostasy, *irtidād* in Arabic, a term stemming from a particular historical situation, the *ridda,* the rebellion of Arab tribes against *islām*—that is, against the community as it existed immediately after the death of the prophet Muhammad.

Like *kufr,* the concept of apostasy refers to a typically Islamic way of seeing things. Nevertheless, the problem is characteristic of all three Abrahamic religions. From a doctrinal and institutional point of view, the religion that proved to be the most rigid and the best "armed" in that respect was not Islam; it was without a doubt Christianity. Given the precariousness of its intermediate position in history, Christianity had to prove its supremacy over the other monotheistic religions by stressing that Judaism had come before it and that Islam had come after it. It was only in Christianity that orthodoxy was defined by dogmas, some of which were summed up in a profession of faith, a "symbol." That symbol was even incorporated into the Christian rite, as the Nicene creed uttered during Mass. Dogmas were formulated and confirmed by councils, and the councils were in turn legitimated by an institution, the Church. The Church dispensed salvation; anyone who repudiated it forfeited redemption. As a result, heretics could be denied a place within the Church and could even be denied the use of the word "Christian," as was the case with the Gnostics. Eventually, the Church laid claim to what was called the secular arm. In 1215, the fourth Lateran council obliged secular authorities to take measures against the Cathari. The noun "Cathari," in fact, is the source of the German word for heretic, *Ketzer*.

Neither Islam nor Judaism has ever had a church. Above all, both lacked the concept of redemption, a founding concept for the Christian Church. In Islam, there exists no special category of individuals, no special profession, whose task it is to dispense salvation; all Muslims are laypersons. There is also no universal creed other than the *shahāda*, which consists in reciting, "There is no god but God, and Muhammad is His messenger." From time to time, theologians or *muhaddithūn* (specialists in the traditions or sayings of the Prophet, hadith) did write professions of faith (*'aqā'id*) that can be compared to the Christian creed, but these texts entailed no obligation and remained valid only for a circumscribed time and place. No official institution ever constrained secular authorities to persecute heretics, though that did not prevent particular governments from becoming guardians of orthodoxy. It must be conceded that everything I have said so far has no direct and necessary consequence for the analysis of actual practices. It is perfectly possible to think dogmatically without having dogmas, and I will not venture to argue that laypersons are any less fanatical than members of the clergy. Islam as well as Christianity has an impressive record of executions, pogroms, and burned books. The systematic and structural differences I have described are real, but they were eclipsed by the prevalence of a trait characteristic of all Abrahamic religions: the devotion demanded by revelation. All these religions belonged to the same family, as it were. Still, we must always keep the differences in mind. In what follows, therefore, I shall speak of the small but significant difference.

What is perceived as a systematic difference is only the result of a historical evolution. Neither the Gospels nor the Koran establishes a system. The content of the faith was defined later, through the work of exegesis. Although, when compared to the New Testament, the Koran is much more explicit in its rules and prescriptions, it does not contain a list of canonical doctrines. Even when it comes closest to an enumeration of prescribed truths, in the verse known as *Āyat al-birr* (sura 2:177), there is a different emphasis: "Righteousness [*birr*] does not consist in whether you face towards the East or the West. The righteous man is he who believes in God and the Last Day, in the angels and the Book and the prophets; who, though he loves it dearly, gives away his wealth to kinsfolk, to orphans, to the destitute, to the traveller in need and to beggars, and for the redemption of captives; who attends to his prayers and renders the alms levy."[3] This verse does not read like a doctrine, an 'aqīda, but is rather a nice mix of statements of faith and charitable practices. The scripture emphasizes "the difference between the formal act of turning toward God and the acceptance of the existential consequences of that act."[4] The doctrinal details mentioned in this verse—God, the Last Judgment, the angels, the Book, the prophets—were never placed in doubt, but they were also never a focus of interest. From the beginning, theology was concerned with altogether different problems: free will and predestination, the attributes of divinity, justification by faith. On the whole, taken in relation to Christianity, Islam did not treat new problems; it treated the same problems differently.[5]

Nevertheless, it would be wrong to say there was no doctrinal progress in Islam. That is far from the case. Over the long term, however, that progress occurred in jurisprudence rather than in dogmatics.

That is the most important thing Muslims learned from their sacred text: how to conduct themselves in an honest and upright manner. The Prophet himself had the opportunity to lay the social and political foundations of his community in Medina. To that end, he was able to make use of what the Koran offered him—namely, a law.

Here again, we find the minor difference. For Islam, orthopraxy is more important than orthodoxy. At the level of action, in the liturgy and in daily life, details counted a great deal. Anyone who wanted to emphasize the unity of the faith by designating Muslims as such, irrespective of their denomination, called them *ahl al-salāt,* that is, "all who pray in the Muslim manner," or *ahl al-qibla,* because they all turned in the same direction *(qibla)* to pray.[6] The law, like Christian dogma, presupposes a distinction between true and false. But a jurist often has to confront the fact that truth presents itself as a matter of circumstance. There are times when the *qibla* cannot be determined, yet the prayer remains valid. The jurist always knows that the truth is not easy to find in a concrete case. Judgment, as his colleagues the *fuqahā'* said, can attain only probability, never certainty. In principle, this could be seen as an appeal for caution.

Nonetheless, scripture also asserted that disagreement was harmful. The Jews and the Christians had sown division in the world; that is why the new revelation was necessary. In the beginning, humankind had been a "single community" *(umma wāhida)*, and God had sent his messengers to maintain its cohesion. But no one followed his advice, and Islam came into being to restore the primordial state of the community. "Had your Lord pleased, He would have made all humanity a single community. They are still at odds, except for those to whom your Lord has shown mercy. To this end He has created them" (sura 11:118; [translation modified]). The early Muslims pondered that verse a great deal. They were obviously the ones "to whom your Lord has shown mercy"; that is why he had spared them antagonism, division. But reality quickly took a different course. With the first civil war, the "Great Discord" in Hishem Djaït's expression, the community split apart. As yet, this event had nothing to do with the doctrine of Islam: it was a political dispute. The first major conquests, however, had convinced the Muslims that they would always be victorious, thanks to the unity God willed for them. Did the *fitna* now mean that, in spite of everything, Muslims were "created" to remain divided, just as the Jews and Christians had been? Initially, people thought they could arrest that pernicious tendency. "Do something about this community before it turns against itself over scripture, as happened to the Jews and Christians," Hudhayfa b. al-Yamān is supposed to have told 'Uthmān, a caliph who would be murdered precisely because he had failed to respond to the rift. The statement is not authentic; it was formulated after the fact, when Muslims realized they were condemned to live in a state of discord. As a result, they made a virtue of necessity and discovered a kind of inter-Muslim pluralism. The Koran did not shed much light on that question. But they were able to turn to the Prophet, whose famous hadith was beginning to circulate: "In my community, disagreement is a sign of divine mercy"; or, to restore its original sense: "In my community, disagreement is *an opportunity* for divine mercy." To this we ought to add, "in contrast to earlier religious communities." It is no accident that this maxim repeats exactly the key words found in the Koranic verse previously cited: "disagreement," "community," "mercy." Hence, though the Muslims were no doubt "created" to be in disagreement, just as all other communities had been, in Islam that same disagreement could be understood in the sense of "diversity." It was something good.[7]

Nevertheless, the hadith I quoted was accepted only in the field of jurisprudence. Divine mercy had manifested itself in the plurality of legal solutions that the *sahāba*, or Companions of the Prophet, had proposed. The fact that this first generation had failed at the political level was ignored. Nevertheless, even in the legal realm, people were not always inclined to accept the disagreements among the Companions as something positive. The Muʿtazilite theologian an-Nazzām did not hesitate to treat their legal positions with caustic irony.[8] But the next stages of Muslim law culminated in such a glorification of the ancestors that they seemed to have become incapable of serious error. This led to the birth of the *sunnah nabawiyya*, the Prophetic tradition, which always left choices to the individual. The space that would later be occupied by legal options or schools, *madhāhib*, was created only by virtue of the Companions' dissent. Islam never had a uniform law, and a jurist could, at least theoretically, always allow himself to turn away from received opinion and adopt one of the minority views held during the first generation. Muslim law is a law of jurists; that is why it took a casuistic form, and why there was never a universally constraining code enforced by a sovereign.

*   *   *

Here again we are faced with one of those minor differences. The Justinian Code and the *Codex Iuris Canonici* taught Christianity that, in jurisprudence as in theology, there was a single fixed system and that it could no longer be called into question. Conversely, in Muslim law, even during the Ottoman Empire, there existed only an intention, a plan, a professorial exegesis of certain fundamental texts carefully chosen according to the consensus of a school. Let us recall in this context that most theologians were trained as jurists; they may therefore have come to the realization that even in the field of theology it was better not to restrict choice excessively. Quite early on, one of them, 'Ubaydallāh al-'Anbarī, judge and governor of Basra, expressed that idea in the form of a maxim. *Kull mutjahid musīb,* he said: "Whoever forms a reasoned opinion is right." He meant not only that the judgment he pronounced as a *qādī* (judge) was valid in all cases and allowed for no judicial review but also that anyone who expressed his own opinion in matters of faith was free to defend it—as was any detractor who reached a different conclusion.[9] It must be admitted, however, that in theology this liberal position did not prevail. That is because theology, unlike jurisprudence, was concerned with eternal truths and not with everyday matters.

For that reason, theological disagreement would very quickly take the form of scandal.

This is brought home to us once again in a saying of the Prophet. It is certainly apocryphal, like the one previously quoted, but it responds to the same question: "My community will have experiences similar to those of the Israelites . . . The Israelites were divided into seventy-two sects, but my community will be divided into seventy-three sects, and all but one will go to hell." No trace remains of the idea that disagreement could be a sign of divine mercy. Rather, the tone of the hadith is one of resignation, as if the truth belonged only to a minority. The desire to protect the community from decadence is obvious. Muslims were therefore glad to be able to quote the Prophet, who claimed: "My community will never reach agreement on an error." The truth will prevail— such was the message. For that reason, Muslims were told, "Abide by the majority view!" The truth, it had to be admitted, was only one among seventy-three opinions, and yet the majority seemed able to distinguish it from the many errors.[10]

At this stage, no sign of the small difference mentioned earlier is in evidence. Muslims had learned that heresy had many faces, yet it was considered aberrant and isolated. For some time, in fact, events proceeded along what would seem to be the normal course, with trials and executions. They were not set in motion by jurists but by the rulers: the caliph and his representatives. The sources tell us whom these measures were directed against: Ghaylān al-Dimashqī, Jaʿd b. Dirham, Jahm b. Safwān, and later, al-Hallāj. In one particular case, that of Bishr al-Marīsī, they even tell us how and where the trial took place: in the courtyard of a mosque, with the participation of a large, probably raging, crowd (even though the *qāḍī* allowed the accused to escape).[11] But in many cases, the essentials are not mentioned. The first trials seem to have been political; but who would be surprised about that? What emerged was the temptation associated with any conviction, religious or not, that is held by the majority—namely, to use violence and to secure the support of the government. The minority sects did not have that opportunity. The Ibadites, for example, and later the Druze, could not execute heretics; they excommunicated and repudiated them until the heretics publicly repented and were again accepted into the community. For the period I am discussing, recourse to violence was not yet the most notable feature. The most important thing for our purposes is that those who staged the trials came to realize what Islam meant to them. There was as yet no orthodoxy; those who would later be called Sunnis still had to determine the content of the sunna, the established custom. Hence the heresy trials also marked stages in the self-definition process of the faith.

As an example, let me cite an execution that took place in Damascus near the middle of the second century AH. The victim was one Muhammad b. Sa 'īd al-Urdunnī, a traditionalist *(muhaddith)* who had questioned the irrevocability of Muhammad's prophethood. As is well known, the Prophet considered himself a link in a chain of messengers, someone who confirmed a revelation that God had "brought down" several times since Creation. With his own preaching Muhammad placed his seal *(khātam)* on that ancient revelation—that is, he bore witness to its truth and authenticity. That does not automatically mean he was the last to place his seal on it. The chain could have continued, and in fact in the early generations, certain people claimed the right to prophesy or were considered prophets. Prophecy had been a unique event on the Arabian Peninsula, but its passing with the death of Muhammad also gave rise to a sense of frustration. For a short time, even 'Umar could not manage to believe it had ended. But prophecy always led to a change—one accomplished by an irrefutable authority—and Islam would have contradicted itself had it given credence to the idea that someone in the future would act toward Islam as Muhammad had acted toward Judaism and Christianity. For that reason, the Koranic formulation that called Muhammad the seal of the prophets was accompanied by the statement that there would be no prophet after him *(lā nabiyya baʿdahū)*. The Damascene theologian, as it happens, now added *in shāʾa 'llāh* (if it be God's will). That is why he was crucified. In a sense, his reaction was altogether logical: it is surely up to God to decide whether he wants to send another messenger. But that objection could not eradicate the scandal.[12]

The sources claim that the word used to designate heresy in this case was *zandaqa,* a term that became widespread shortly thereafter. But the term was at first reserved for a very specific heresy, dualism. The *zanādiqa* were initially Manichaeans or Muslims attracted to that Iranian doctrine. In reality, the attraction Manichaeanism exerted over Muslims had little to do with dualism. What Muslim intellectuals appreciated above all was its scientific modernity. That may seem astonishing today. The image of Manichaeanism that emerges from the Greek texts, the

works of Saint Augustine, and the original Mani-
chaean writings discovered in the meantime is totally
different, that of a bizarre mythology and a harsh
and rigid vegetarian asceticism. But in the Near East,
Manichaeanism came to be known for its cosmological speculations. For the Manichaeans, the world
originated from the mixing of two eternal principles,
light and shadow; therein lay the Iranian solution to
the problem of creation. The category of mixture was
reminiscent of an element of Hellenistic philosophy:
the Stoic idea of *krasis di' holou, tadākhul,* as the
Muʿtazilite an-Nazzām would have said, an idea that
had permeated Iranian thought long before.[13] This
was a sort of natural science whose hypothetical
character made it ideal for educated people inclined
to speculate without examining things closely. The
fact that this system was defended by dualists was
not important in itself. Muslim intellectuals, Manichaeans, and thinkers with similar leanings (dualists
who embraced Bardesanes's system, alchemists, and
so on) all belonged to the same circle. But outside
that circle, the curiosity they displayed for such ideas
left a bad impression. The simple people, who understood Islam differently, and the scholars in the traditionalist camp, the *ashāb al-hadīth,* took a dim view
of such speculations. Under Caliph al-Mahdī, the

government responded, conducting investigations and dismissing officials, since most of the "crypto-Manichaeans" worked for the government.[14]

The sources have somewhat more to say in this case. Nevertheless, details of the events elude us. We have no trial transcripts, and the accounts are rarely reliable or contemporary with the events. In general, it appears that heretics were not sentenced to death. But for a certain period of time a new position was created, that of inquisitor *(sāhib al-zanādiqa)*. The situation was thus taken seriously. From that point on, it became clear that Manichaeanism was not compatible with Islam. Even during the persecution, the term *zandaqa,* dualist heresy, had been used by intellectuals to slander one another.[15] Shortly thereafter, the same word became a legal term. Henceforth, anyone who committed *zandaqa* merited the death sentence. The only question remaining open was whether the condemned ought to have an opportunity to repent before being executed. In legal terms, that procedure was more or less logical and consistent, since it respected the profession of faith *lā ilāha illā 'llāh* (there is no god but God) of the *shahāda,* which is taken from the Koran (sura 37:35). The second half of that profession of faith is also in the Koran (sura 48:29). We do not know at what point the two expressions were brought together, but it was fairly early, long before the trial in Damascus in any case. Coins minted under ʿAbd al-Malik ibn Marwān are already inscribed with the *shahāda*. Henceforth it would become the eternal symbol of Islamic identity.

The foreign origin of *zandaqa* was obvious to any Arab who heard the word pronounced. Its morphology left no doubt that it was Persian. *Zindīq* is derived from *zand*, the commentary on the Avesta. By the Sassanid era, the Manichaeans had acquired the dubious reputation of developing a very personal exegesis of Mazdean doctrine.[16] At first, that did not matter much to Muslims. The Umayyads had tolerated the Manichaeans and had even used them to oppose the old Sassanid bureaucracy. But when the Abbasids moved the center of the Syrian empire to Iraq and founded the new capital of Baghdad near the ruins of ancient Ctesiphon, things took a different turn, and in the ensuing persecutions the defamatory term the Sassanids had invented was put to use. Most Arabs knew nothing of its etymology, and soon the sources applied it to every sort of heretical deviation. In the end, however, the word came to designate something more than a simple error—namely, unbelief. For that reason, the punishment had to be the one reserved for apostasy.

It was at that point that theologians joined the fray. It was primarily jurists who were responsible for meting out punishment, whereas theologians were supposed to be concerned with defining heresy and refuting the arguments of its proponents. The authorities wanted to know when exactly mere error became unbelief. Quite often, heresiography was not merely theoretical. By producing a list of deviations, it offered categories that could be used to establish measures for prevention and persecution. We can assume that, when these events were occurring under Caliph al-Mahdī, theologians played the role of attack dogs for Islam, with the approval if not the encouragement of the government. We know that several of them, still young and ambitious, wrote pamphlets against the supporters of *zandaqa*.[17] Early on, they also began to make vicious attacks on one another. At first they played fair, engaging in debates and disputations, but gradually they became more aggressive. Those who built a protective wall around Islam were obliged to indicate what would remain outside it, and as a result monotheism and Muhammad's prophecies were no longer understood as the only criteria for truth. Theologians believed in the power of reason, since they could not conduct a debate with unbelievers by appealing to the Koran or to tradition. In addition, they were nearly certain they would prevail in these interreligious controversies. Since they were "in the right," the possibility of failure was practically ruled out. Unprovable or inexplicable facts, "mysteries" as a Christian would have called them, do not seem to have existed. That is why they had no scruples about arguing, even within their own camp, that their way of understanding Islam was the only valid one. They were rationalists and as such were always sure of themselves. Hence, when the opinions expressed by one of their colleagues became too personal, theologians tended to call them "unbelief" as well. In a sense, these were only words. They simply meant: Whoever believes in such things will certainly be damned. Unlike the cases previously mentioned, these verbal attacks did not generally put in jeopardy the physical well-being of those being criticized. But the polemics contained the seed of radicalization. Indeed, the theologians, both Mu'tazilites and others, sometimes tried to hand the dissidents over to the police. That is what happened to the Mu'tazilite al-Mu'ammar[18] and later to his colleague Ibn al-Rāwandi.[19]

Here, then, was the notorious *takfir* (anathema). But what was the source of the aversion toward that attitude? One answer is that it is already found in the Koran, in the words *lā ikrāha fī 'l-dīn* (no compulsion in religion) of sura 2:256. But that argument was never made in classical Islam, and the verse cited did not play a notable role. The decisive factor in the restraint of medieval Muslims was instead a historical event: Khārijism. The Khārijites were the first to practice the anathema and, for that reason, bad memories were always associated with them. They considered themselves the only true Muslims. They did so in the first place for reasons more political than religious, but they were intent on reproducing the Prophet's exemplary migration *(hijrah)*, and they withdrew to regions where they could live alone, in the desert or on the periphery of the Muslim world. That schism resulted from the claim to exclusive sanctity. Hence the Khārijites abhorred intermarriage with non-Khārijite Muslims. They also battled their coreligionists everywhere they could. They believed they were dealing not with Muslims of lesser quality but quite simply with unbelievers, who, moreover, had knowingly rejected the true faith. Because of that postulate, they were able to apply to their coreligionists everything that had been said in the Koran about the pagans. As a result, not only were they convinced that all other Muslims would go to hell, but they

30

even felt justified in conducting a jihad against them. The majority of believers considered them not only extremist schismatics, but also thugs *(bughāt)* and terrorists. That image of them persisted even after they had become peaceful communities or had completely disappeared from entire regions. From that time on, it was the norm to identify the practice of *takfīr* with exclusivism and extremism.

The court theologians I mentioned, Mu'tazilites for the most part, took that fact into consideration. They carefully refrained from cutting themselves off from the community; they wanted only to define the creed more precisely. The doctrines they hated most were anthropomorphism and predestination. These, they thought, crossed the line into unbelief. But they inevitably found themselves in disreputable company because of the language they used. Their adversaries saw their suspicions confirmed when the Mu'tazilites became involved in a campaign of religious persecution, the *mihna*, which somewhat served the Mu'tazilites' goals. This inquisition had been unleashed by the caliph. I will not comment further on it.[20] What matters in this context is simply that the theologians were on the side of the persecutors. They added a certain arrogance to the state's action. They were shameless in pointing out to the victims that they owed their situation to their stupidity, which had led them astray. No one was executed, and as for the circumstances that led Ahmad b. Hanbal, the most distinguished victim—at least in the light of later tradition—to be flogged during a disputation, they are still much debated.[21] The caliph did, however, try to paralyze the entire "system" of opponents, by barring their jurists from practicing their profession. Not only were the judges dismissed, but the muftis, who were consulted by devout commoners in religious matters, were forbidden to practice. That decision was considered scandalous because those who worked in the legal system, including professional witnesses—indispensable for the verification of all official documents—were notables, *probi homines*. The common people took the victims' side; the persecution was perceived as an ordeal, a tribulation *(mihna)*. And the court theologians completely lost touch with the masses.

Matters took a bad turn. Fifteen years later, the government measures had to be revoked. That event would be a key experience for the Sunni world, and it is still commemorated in many popular accounts. The people had won a victory over the authorities, or at least that was the impression. The devout victims were considered martyrs for a just cause. The caliph had lost the battle, and henceforth any religious policy conducted by the government was unlikely to gain the necessary support. From that time on, specialists in the Prophetic tradition, *ashāb al-hadīth*, came to form a separate bloc. Their role was to interpret divine law and to decide whether to cooperate with the government. Theology was discredited; its representatives had abused reason by exerting pressure on those who held views contrary to their own. The hateful aspect of anathema *(takfīr)*, the anxiety it produced, is mentioned in the historical accounts. It was associated with a negative view of all theological and dialectical argument. Once more, what matters is the perception of history, the *Geschichtsbild*, the image engraved in collective memory. It took time for that evolution to occur, and rational theology never completely died out. But for many, dialectical thought now had a bad reputation. It could be understood as eristic, and anathematizing was assimilated to arrogance and presumptuousness. As a result, theology was not deemed the loftiest of the sciences, as it was in the Christian Middle Ages—philosophy even less so. It was jurisprudence that became the premier discipline. Here again we are faced with the small but significant difference. In Islam, religious expertise remained in the hands of those who were later called the ulema, a group of middle-class scholars who explained the faith on the basis of an exegesis of the Koran to others of the same class and who solved everyday problems with their legal advice. As it happens, the criterion they used to reestablish order was consensus, a term I use in its sociological sense and not in the limited sense it has assumed in Islamic religious law.

That social consensus was never institutionalized. It was not officially sanctioned by synods or councils, for there was no one to invoke such things. The "system"—if we may call it that—was extremely informal. Every properly trained jurist had the right to pronounce legal opinions based on certain presuppositions, and the minority view was a sign of divine mercy, as explained earlier. Naturally, the margin of freedom in the decision was limited by the growth of consensus, but given that a legal consensus, *ijmā'*, was established only after the fact, it did not exert its full power to clinch matters until after society itself had given its approval. The question of which movement constituted a sect and which did not was decided not by dogma but by the views of the local majority or the minority's lack of success. Persecution was a matter not of definitions and laws, but of circumstances and temperament. Nevertheless, the situation was far from ideal. The Hanbalites, former victims of the inquisition and their successors, gave their adversaries a taste of their own medicine. Their self-defense organizations *('aiyyārūn, ahdāth)* carried their reign of terror into enemy neighborhoods. With all the more reason, deviationists in their own camp were forced to retract their opinions.

But social tolerance was preserved nonetheless. The jurists were interested primarily in what someone had done, not in what someone had thought. Until evidence to the contrary surfaced, they felt obliged to hold a good opinion *(husn al-zann)* of every coreligionist, because any sin committed remained a matter between the sinner and God, so long as it did not harm anyone. Naturally, the danger always existed that a theologian or jurist would stir up the masses against someone who had a bad reputation— a reprobate, an adversary—or against a dissident group. But when the government wanted to make an example of someone, it had first to establish an *ijmā',* a consensus of jurists, and normally that did not happen unless several fatwas had been pronounced by different legal schools (as in the case of al-Hallāj). In general, the secular authorities were interested less in suppressing heresy than in avoiding the popular uprisings that resulted from them, and it was very rare for the ulema, who were responsible for the spiritual realm, to ask for help from the secular arm, as the Christian Church did.

It is no simple matter to describe the mechanisms at work here. The important thing to remember is that almost nothing was officially regulated. Someone whose "orthodoxy" was considered suspect was treated with a certain coolness. Fathers were unlikely to allow a daughter to marry him; neighbors would often not visit him when he was sick; few would attend his funeral. Above all, people were hesitant to greet such a person, for the greeting always took the form of a blessing, and the devout tended to save their blessings for those who shared their faith. As a matter of fact, that was also the case with the Jewish "shalom." So long as someone was not considered a member of one's own faith, one simply *returned* the greeting, and not always in a friendly way. A scholar who was not orthodox could be boycotted; when he no longer had any students, his books would no longer be copied. When an unpopular preacher was dismissed or driven out, his pulpit was sluiced out to cleanse it. In addition, one could show respect by praying behind a particular person, for there were enough mosques to allow each Muslim to choose his own imam. It was only on Friday that everyone went to the main mosque, where the caliph or his representative led the prayer. Only at that time were some people liable to act against their personal convictions. During funerals, the social rank of the person who uttered the prayer over the body revealed what was thought of the orthodoxy of the deceased. Even in the major cities, personal reputation did not lose its importance; people lived in segmentary societies where modern anonymity was still unknown. As for scholars, the value judgments applied to them have been preserved in a rich body of biographical literature, and the criteria were always religious.[22]

These value judgments were conservative. It could hardly be otherwise in a society founded on consensus. Communal harmony was more important than originality. In doctrine and in personal behavior, Muslims leaned toward a generally accepted middle ground. Against that backdrop, both the major Islamic denominations chose terms to designate those who deviated from the norm. They were "exaggerators" *(ghulāt)*, Shiites said, when they no longer wanted to be associated with the idiosyncrasies of their own past.[23] They introduced innovations *(ahdāth, bidaʿ)*, said the Sunnis, contrasting the heretics' attitude to their own traditionalism. In a sense, the term "innovation" captures the mindset of any religion that, on account of revelation, has its apogee at the beginning. The Byzantines spoke of *neoterismōs* and Tertullian alluded to the *novellitas* of the sectarians. The Latin text that provided Christian theology with its popular definition of orthodoxy, Vincent of Lérins's *Commonitorium,* bears the subtitle "Defense of the Antiquity and Universality of the Catholic Faith against the Impious *Innovations* of All Heretics." The notion contained a good dose of criticism of the present and nostalgia for the good old days, an attitude one finds everywhere and in every era. That said, the Sunnis were to a certain degree predisposed to such an attitude. Over against the notion of *bid'a* was always its opposite, sunna, or ancient custom, which was legitimated by the Prophet's authority. That is why the term "innovation" ultimately designated not only doctrinal aberration but also, and to an even greater degree, reprehensible practices: additions to the ritual prayer, immoderation in reciting the Koran, popular customs practiced during Ramadan or religious holidays, excesses in expressing grief, or women's participation at funeral ceremonies.[24]

In typically Muslim fashion, people paid more attention to orthopraxy than to orthodoxy. That is also why what was new one day could be old the next.

Dogmas can become ossified and resist any change in language or point of view; certain phrases from the Christian creed are a good example. The innovations Islam spoke of were something else again: at one time, coffee and tobacco were innovations and were attacked with many theological and legal arguments. A little later, however, everyone accepted their use. Hence, people began early on to differentiate between innovations that were good and those which were bad or, to express it in the jurists' refined vocabulary, between innovations that were deplorable, those which were permitted, and those which were recommended. It would have been impossible to use the terms "good" or "bad" with respect to heresies. As a result, even the most unacceptable innovation stemmed not from rebellion against God but from mental confusion. It could and ought to meet with disapproval, but no legal measures should be taken.

In this context, it may be advisable to cite a great theologian, al-Ghazālī (AH 450–505; 1058–1111 CE). In his *Tahāfut al-falāsifa,* al-Ghazālī had indicated the point at which the philosophers' doctrines degenerated into unbelief; he thus knew whereof he spoke. But a few years later, after a spiritual crisis that made him doubt the omnipotence of reason and of intellectual squabbles, he wrote a treatise on the distinction between Islam and *zandaqa* in which he warned his readers against hasty use of the term *kufr* (heresy).[25] Unbelief, he said, is a purely legal category. A Christian would never have said that. Al-Ghazālī could defend that formulation because he knew that unbelief entails certain consequences. For example, no one can inherit from an unbeliever, and an unbeliever can be killed if not under the protection of a Muslim authority. But, added al-Ghazālī, that applies only to Muslim apostates, and one commits apostasy only when one denies the essential dogmas: monotheism, Muhammad's prophecy, and the Last Judgment. That short list once again conforms to the *shahāda*. The only thing that has been added is the Last Judgment, which naturally implies acceptance of the divine commandments. But only the person who entirely rejects the Law, that is, the antinomian, is an unbeliever. Al-Ghazālī wrote a treatise against the antinomian current, or *ibāhiyya*.

In that book, *Faysal al-tafriqa*, al-Ghazālī also took the opportunity to argue in favor of reconciliation and restraint. He knew that Sunnis and Shiites had a hard time coexisting, but he recommended that anyone accused of heresy not return the insult, for God is generous toward human beings and one must al-

ways follow his example. Of course, everything depends on the way one interprets scripture; false exegesis, *ta'wīl*, is at the root of every deviation and
aberration. But one must always abide by unanimous
agreement, and if someone does not bow to it, one
must remember that consensus does not include
everyone. It is not fixed, and it is not the same everywhere and always. Granted, only one of the seventy-
three Muslim sects will achieve salvation, according
to the famous Prophetic tradition quoted earlier. But
that hadith, al-Ghazālī added, is not reliable; a variant of it is to be preferred. According to that variant,
only one of the seventy-three groups that constitute
Islam will perish. Al-Ghazālī thus went a long way in
his defense of tolerance and peace. He did not hesitate to change one of the Prophet's sayings that
seemed to justify those who thought they had a monopoly on salvation, and he did so in such a way as to
express the hope that almost all Muslims would ultimately be saved. In al-Ghazālī's time, the majority of
Muslims, those we now call Sunnis, had stopped believing that any of the groups of the *ahl al-qibla* would
be eternally damned; rather, all would ultimately be
saved by the *shahāda*. Even heretics and innovators
had only a kind of purgatory to fear. In addition,
even if a true unbeliever sinned because he was igno-

rant of Islam, he would be forgiven by God, said al-Ghazālī.

We may wonder to what extent al-Ghazālī, despite his renown, represents Islam as such. It is beyond question that what he said represented first and foremost a postulate—theory and not reality. And yet in the tradition in which al-Ghazālī was trained, al-Ash'arī is reported to have asserted at the time of his death: "I attest that I anathematize none of my brothers (the *ahl al-qibla*), for they all call on the same God; the differences are only verbal." It is possible that these words are apocryphal; others were also attributed to the dying al-Ash'arī. Nevertheless, the fact that they are cited is in itself revealing, for al-Ash'arī, like al-Ghazālī, represents the middle ground and avoids the extremes of the two major persecutions: the anathemas of the Mu'tazilite inquisitors and those of their Hanbalite victims. That attitude became the guiding principle for later Sunni theology.[26] Ricoldo da Montecroce, a Dominican monk who traveled to the Orient near the end of the thirteenth century, was outraged that Muslims did not follow the maxim that narrow is the way to salvation, because, he said, "even when they do no more than recite that 'there is no god but God and Muhammad is his messenger,' for them that means they will surely achieve salvation. All the Saracens agree with the view that a Saracen need only say that and he shall be saved, even if he has committed all the sins in the world. In spite of the fact that their law, the Koran, has established a goodly number of prohibitions, the sinner will suffer no punishment. . . . We can therefore call their law permissive. Satan in his malice saw to it that those who do not achieve bliss by taking the straight and narrow way will take the wide road to hell."[27]

There is reason to wonder whether, in the end, that wide road was not the better one. Strictly speaking, Islam had no religious wars like those in Europe. But Islam can be as militant as Christianity; the danger of making religion into an ideology exists everywhere. Those who assault the dignity of the Prophet, even without denying him directly—the Bahā'īs and the Ahmadiyya because they postulate another divine messenger after him, Salman Rushdie because he defames the person of Muhammad through literary parody—are sure to incur the wrath of the majority. It seems that "heresy" is now defined in relation to Muhammad's prophethood and sanctity, rather than by the *tawhīd*—that is, the concept of God's oneness. More emphasis is placed on the second half of the *shahāda* than on the first. We may wonder about the reasons for that change in perspective. For al-Ghazālī in his *Tahāfut al-falāsifa*, that was not yet the case. The fear of heresy has certainly not disappeared; we are witness to new orthodoxies created by the media, Saudi money, and politico-religious movements. But that phenomenon will have to be dealt with elsewhere. With regard to classical Islam, we can say that in spite of everything the jurists, however suspect they may have become for us, treated the question with more flexibility than we would expect from theologians or, to speak of our own time, from politicians. The "innovations" they felt obliged to stigmatize did not condemn anyone to be burned at the stake. But like "deviations" and "counterrevolutions" in our own day, the "unbelief" that was the object of theologians' polemics was a much more unpleasant companion.

2

THEOLOGY AND THE KORAN

The Mi'rāj and the Debate on Anthropomorphism

THE ASCENSION TO HEAVEN was an experience shared by Jesus and Muhammad, that is, by the religious imagination of Christianity and of Islam. But the two instances have totally different contexts. For Christians, Jesus' ascension was the logical consequence of the resurrection. The Koran, however, does not speak of resurrection. According to it, Jesus rose to heaven directly from the cross, without dying on it. And when Muhammad ascended to heaven, he did not remain there, but returned to earth. His ascension marked the beginning of his career; it was then that he learned what task he was to perform, and the success of that task would be obvious to everyone in his community. By contrast, at the time of his ascension, Jesus had completed his earthly mission and, in fact, had apparently failed. In returning to heaven, he showed that, despite his crucifixion, he belonged to the kingdom of God. Let us not forget that it is only in Western languages that the term "ascension" is applied to both events. In Arabic, there are two: for the Prophet, the word used is *mi'rāj*, whereas Jesus is "lifted" to heaven, *rafaʿahū 'llāh ilayhi*, the Koran says (sura 4:158; compare 3:55). Muslims never compared Muhammad to Jesus in that regard. That fact is all the more glaring, given that comparisons in general were not lacking, at least in the first phase of Islam, as attested in hadith. But these comparisons, which were based on purely Koranic ideas, referred to other prophets: Abraham, it was said at the time, was the friend of God *(khalīl Allāh),* Moses the one to whom God had spoken on Mount Sinai *(kalīm Allāh),* and Muhammad, finally, the one who ascended to heaven, where he saw God in person. This was more than a comparison, it was a tripartite schema of increasing intimacy: being close to God (Abraham), hearing his voice (Moses), seeing his countenance (Muhammad). That schema presented the situation in a new form, which also raised specific problems.

I will not deal with accounts of the *mi'rāj* as such. They are well known, and for those who do not remember the texts, the Persian miniatures that evoke them stand as a reminder.[1] Let me emphasize one point, however. As I have said, Muhammad did not remain in heaven. He was not reunited with God after being sent to earth for a time. In reality, what happened was that he had an audience with God. And that audience had a particular aim: God prescribed the number of prayers his community was supposed to say every day. At first, the Almighty was quite demanding: he spoke of fifty prayers. Muhammad had to bargain, and he managed to reduce the number to five. This reminds us of the scene in the Old Testament in which Abraham also bargains on behalf of the righteous who live in Sodom and Gomorrah and who are spared by God when he lets "loose . . . a shower of claystones," as the Koran says (sura 11:82). It was Moses who advised the Prophet to bargain; Muhammad had encountered him during his journey through the heavenly spheres. Moses and Abraham were the last two prophets Muhammad saw, those closest to God in their cosmic role—and those with whom he was compared in the tripartite schema I mentioned.

We can imagine the fascination these tales exerted on the public at the time. They had one major defect, however. At first glance, nothing of what they related could be found in scripture proper. In the Koran, the word *mi'rāj* appears only once, in sura 70, where God is called *dhū 'l-ma'ārij,* Lord of the Ladders. The text continues: "The angels and the Spirit will ascend to Him in one day: a day whose space is fifty thousand years." But that is something other than the *mi'rāj;* the Prophet is not mentioned. As a result, exegetes had to search for other evidence, and in fact they never relied on the passage cited, but rather on two others, also found in the Koran. First, there is the famous verse in sura 17: "Glory be to Him who made His servant go by night from the Sacred Temple to the farther Temple [*masjid al-aqsā*] whose surroundings We have blessed, that We might show him of our signs." It is an isolated verse, and what follows offers no further clarifications. But the word "signs" *(āyātinā)* could be interpreted as an allusion to ascension or to vision. And given the qualifier, the *masjid al-aqsā,* the "final place of veneration," found in a place "whose surroundings we have blessed" could be located in the Holy Land, in Jerusalem. Under the Umayyad dynasty, a mosque built in that city came to be called al-Masjid al-aqsā. Muhammad had traveled by night to Jerusalem—that was the conclusion exegetes drew. It was not yet an ascension in the strict sense, for Muhammad's journey was horizontal, not vertical. True, he went to the place where Jesus had ascended to heaven, but Muslims had no desire to compare him to Jesus, as we have seen.

Let us now consider the second passage in the Koran. It is longer, but just as mysterious. It acquired its importance by virtue of the fact that it seemed to contain an allusion to a meeting with God. In the beginning of surat al-Najm (53), the Koran speaks of two visions by the Prophet. These are unusual texts, since normally Muhammad does not see, but hears. The Koran resulted from instances of hearing. The passage is well known:

1. By the declining star,
2. your compatriot is not in error, nor is he mad!
3. His is no language of passion.
4. This is only revelation revealed to him.
5. He is taught by one who is mighty
6. and wise. He stood
7. on the supreme horizon;
8. then, drawing near, he hung suspended
9. within two bows' length or even closer,
10. and revealed to his servant that which he revealed to him.
11. His heart did not lie about what he had seen.

Immediately thereafter comes the account of the second vision:

13. He had seen him come down another time
14. at the sidra tree, beyond which no one may pass.
15. Near it is the Garden of Repose.
16. When that tree was covered with what covered it [him],
17. his eyes did not wander, nor did they turn aside:
18. for he saw one of his Lord's greatest signs.[2]

Once again, then, there is a "sign," as in the case of the *masjid al-aqsā*. That may have led exegetes to combine the two passages. The location of the event is even vaguer than before. But the visions as such are fairly concrete, described in a way that cannot fail to excite curiosity. One striking fact: the account is in the third person. It may be surmised that God spoke in his own voice; he seemed to reveal a secret that no one but the Prophet could have known.

It was not known exactly whom the Prophet saw, however. Those hearing or reading the passage had to decide for themselves. Modern exegetes usually insist on the idea that the Prophet saw Gabriel at that time. But it is practically certain that those responsible for incorporating these verses into the traditions of the *mi'rāj* were convinced that Muhammad had seen God rather than Gabriel. The sight of God was the apogee of the tripartite schema; the audience granted to the Prophet was not limited to a mere perception of the divine voice, as Moses had experienced it on Sinai. The only difficulty was that the concept of God implied by that idea was liable to cause a scandal, since the vision seemed to imply *tashbīh,* anthropomorphism, and the problem of anthropomorphism had concerned Islam ever since Muslims had begun to think about it in theological terms. In Christianity, the question was neutralized by the idea of incarnation. It would be an exaggeration to say that this change in perspective made it easier to understand. It is no accident that Tertullian, the African Church Father, said in his treatise *De carne Christi* (On the flesh of Jesus Christ): *Certum est quia impossibile,* "[the incarnation] is a certainty *because* it is impossible." A Muslim would never have put it that way. In any case, it was not easy to find a rational explanation for God's visibility.

The internal contradictions are pointed out in the Koran itself. A later passage found in surat al-Takwīr contains an allusion to one of the two visions in surat al-Najm: "No, your compatriot is not possessed.

He saw him on the clear horizon" (81:23). There is the same lack of precision: "He saw him." But in a previous verse the person seen is identified as a "venerable and mighty messenger, held in honor by the Lord of the Throne" [translation modified]. It absolutely cannot refer to God; a "venerable messenger" is normally an angel.

Is our problem solved by that parallel? Perhaps it is, for a reader these days, but it was not for the exegetes we are discussing. And for us the question arises on the historical level. Jewish thought already had a tendency to eliminate the scandal of anthropomorphism by taking statements about God to be statements about an angel. The angel Metatron plays that role in certain Talmudic passages. The Kabbalah takes the same tack. The angel could assume the functions of the Creator; it was like a kind of demiurge, "one who is obeyed," *mutāʿ*, as the Muslims said.[3] In fact, the term *mutāʿ* appears in surat al-Takwīr (81:21). The fundamental conditions had changed. The verses in surat al-Takwīr were certainly later than those of surat al-Najm, for now the vision is no longer described in detail, but simply mentioned as something already known. The public addressed in surat al-Takwīr may have lived in Medina, where the Jewish community listened to the Prophet's revelations with a critical ear. In any case, the later passage does not rule out the possibility that previously, in surat al-Najm, it was God that Muhammad thought he had seen. At the end of the first vision, in fact, the text says, of the person who approached the Prophet, that he "revealed to his servant that which he revealed to him." "His servant" (*'abdhū*) can only be understood here as "the servant of God," that is, Muhammad. If that is true, the one who reveals is no longer a "venerable messenger" but God himself, and God would therefore also be the object of the vision.

Nevertheless, we must take one other thing into account: According to the Koran, the Prophet did not see God while the Prophet was in heaven but when he was somewhere on earth. He saw him "on the supreme horizon," and he had seen him, it is said at the beginning of the second vision, "come down another time" (*nazlatan ukhrā*). Hence, it is not the Prophet who rises to God but God who descends to Muhammad. Moreover, it is immediately added that he saw "the sidra tree, beyond which no one may pass" (*sidrat al-muntahā*) and that "near it is the Garden of Repose." That sounds like code for paradise, with "Garden of Repose" (*jannāt al-ma'wā*) designating the place where the blessed will rest during or after the Judgment (see sura 32:19). As for the "sidra tree," it marks the place beyond which no one may pass, the outer boundary of the holy of holies, where God himself dwells. Nevertheless, God could "come down" to that point, since people still thought at the time that paradise was located on earth. It is therefore not necessary for us to embrace the idea earlier defended by a number of Orientalists (from Grimme and Caetani to Richard Bell and Régis Blachère) who saw the Garden of Repose simply as a plantation near Mecca, perhaps a villa, a kind of Monrepos for well-off city folk, and the "sidra tree, beyond which no one may pass" as a tree of some sort found on the borderline of the Mecca sanctuary. In any case, Muslim exegesis never questioned that the encounter had taken place in paradise, though that place was on earth. The "sidra tree, beyond which no one may pass" thus became a kind of emblem of the Prophet's ascension. Even accounts of the ascension that take nothing else from surat al-Najm use that mythical tree to mark the ultimate threshold, seventh heaven. It is there that is located the source of the four rivers of paradise. The exegetical situation was thus becoming rather complex. Two competing alternatives surfaced: God or angel, heaven or earth. That created four possibilities. In addition, we must not forget we are dealing with two visions, not just one. For a single ascension, one of them would have sufficed; but if the Prophet had to bargain with God concerning the number of prayers, two are hardly enough.

Any exegesis whatsoever ratifies a theological decision. Nevertheless, in the present case, as in all the others, it is not the product of a free-floating imagination. Its general orientation comes from models worked out within a local tradition. We know that the motif of the heavenly journey was widespread in the ancient world; an entire body of secondary literature is devoted to it. But this is not the place to elaborate on the question of "influences." What matters is the exegete's existential decision, his *Vorentscheidung*, or prejudgment. Those who were put off by anthropomorphism would soon come to believe that the Prophet had seen Gabriel, and in this world. Muhammad, it was thus supposed, learned of the task he was to perform and received his first revelation from the angel. That is also the reason, as the exegete in question might have gone on to say, that this event is worthy of mention in the Koran. Indeed, at that moment, Gabriel appeared to the Prophet for the first time, and he also revealed his true angelic nature; he was not disguised in human form. The only question still needing to be resolved, then, is why Muhammad saw Gabriel twice. Moreover, at the philological level, one had to address the difficulty of the personal pronoun in the sentence: "He revealed to his servant what he revealed." In spite of this, that view of things was accepted by the majority. It is already found in Ibn Ishāq's biography of the Prophet, composed in Medina in the first half of the second century AH.

Those who adopted that interpretation could not, strictly speaking, reconcile the account of surat al-Najm with the *mi'rāj*. Many were not inclined to accept this circumstance, for no other support for the *mi'rāj* appears in the Koran, and hadith on its own had not yet acquired sufficient authority. But those who insisted on taking the two passages from surat al-Najm as proof of a vision of God could not help wondering how and in what form the Prophet had seen God. The responses given constitute the first evidence we have of theological reflection. They are found in the Prophetic tradition, hadith. The texts reported there are frequently nothing but a sort of disguised exegesis. A chain of transmitters, an *isnād*, precedes each tradition and guarantees its reliability. The example I will cite is of particular interest because the people constituting this *isnād* are incorporated into a sort of frame story:

Yahyā reports: I asked Abū Salama: "What part
of the Koran was revealed first?" He replied:
"You that are wrapped up in your cloak!" (sura
74). I said: "[But] I was told it was "Recite in the
name of your Lord" (sura 96)." Abū Salama replied: "I myself asked the question of Jābir b.
'Abd Allāh, and he said: "You that are wrapped
up in your cloak," and I, like you, replied that I
had been told it was "Recite in the name of your
Lord." [Jābir] then replied: "I can only tell you
what the Messenger of God himself said,
namely: 'I had withdrawn to Mount Hirā' to
meditate [*jāwartu fi Hirā'*]. After completing my
retreat, I descended to the valley floor. Then I
heard a voice calling me. I looked around me,
ahead of me, behind, to the left and to the right;
but [only when I looked upward] . . . *There he
was, seated on his throne, between heaven and earth.* I
immediately returned to Khadīja and told [her]:
Wrap me up and pour cold water over me!'
Then [the revelation] came down to me: 'You
that are wrapped up in your cloak! Arise and
give warning! Magnify your Lord.'"

The story ends with the first verses of sura 74,
God's call, which prepared Muhammad for his pro-

phetic mission. That call is preceded by the vision. But the crucial problem lies elsewhere. Scholars were divided on the identity of the first revelation that "came down" to Muhammad. Was it sura 74 or sura 96? Each camp defended its position by invoking Companions as its authorities; that is why the opinions of each could only take the form of a hadith. The chain of transmitters shows us that the dispute occurred in Medina. There, in the city where the Prophet died, it was thought that the information on his life and experiences was more accurate than elsewhere.

The Prophet thus saw God in all his might and glory seated on his throne. Historians of religion are hardly surprised by that, for we are familiar with that scenario from the Bible and the ancient Orient. When someone wanted to depict God in his majesty, he was shown seated on his throne. But as an interpretation of the vision of surat al-Najm, the image is somewhat surprising, for although the Prophet sees God "on the supreme horizon" ("between heaven and earth," as the hadith says in its exegetical reformulation), according to the Koran he is apparently not seated. Rather, *istawā wa-huwa bi'l-ufuq al-a'lā,* "he stood on the supreme horizon." At this point, we must turn to philology. Translations are always interpretations and, where the Koran is concerned, they still frequently rely on medieval exegesis. The verb *istawā,* "to stand," is ambiguous. It can also signify a seated posture; when the verb is used in the Koran with reference to God, it normally appears in the expression *istawā ʿalā ʾl-ʿarsh,* "God sits upright on his throne." In surat al-Najm, it could be understood the same way. Conversely, the throne was no longer appropriate when the vision was attributed to Gabriel; an angel does not sit on a throne, he stands. He receives orders, he is ready to be sent out as a messenger, but he is not a lord. When he is standing, Ibn Isḥāq tells us, "his feet are next to each other" on the supreme horizon, sort of like an Egyptian statue's, and then he draws near. Yet according to the hadith we are considering, it is rather the throne that draws near. The throne comes down, hovering *(tadallā),* like a pail *(dalw)* into a well, until it is two bows' lengths or even closer *(qāba qawsayni aw adnā).* In that intimate situation, the Prophet, his ear close to God's mouth, receives his first revelation.

More precisely, according to the text, Muhammad did not receive the revelation until he was home, covered by a cloak. But the content of the message received at home corresponds exactly to what he might have previously heard from God's mouth: "Arise and give warning! Magnify your Lord." He is not yet obliged to transmit a particular message; he is quite simply initiated. He must henceforth magnify the Lord, and he learns of that mission after returning home and wrapping himself in his cloak, in order to concentrate. At the time the vision occurred, he was not yet prepared to receive the message; he heard a voice, but he was so dazzled by the apparition that he did not realize the meaning of what he heard.

Let us take this opportunity to pause and recapitulate. Everything that has been said up to now remains hypothetical. The sources are contradictory, and the secondary literature offers incompatible solutions. The first hypothesis is the easiest to defend: In the initial phase of Koranic exegesis, there were people who believed that, consistent with the account of surat al-Najm, Muhammad had seen God, and not Gabriel. As I have pointed out, that contradicts the image of the Prophet presented in his canonical biography. But at the time, Ibn Ishāq's *Sīra* was not yet a canonical book; the positions the author supported were not always identical with those of his contemporaries. One need only consult al-Tabarī's *Tafsīr,* or commentary, to realize this. Al-Tabarī himself did not like anthropomorphism. His skepticism, in fact, led to his being persecuted by the Hanbalites of his time.[4] He therefore interpreted the visions in surat al-Najm as being those of an angel—Gabriel, to be precise. Nevertheless, he cites 'Abdallāh b. 'Abbās and Anas b. Mālik among the Companions of the Prophet who were inclined to believe it was a vision of God, and he also cites 'Ikrima, Ibn 'Abbās's slave and disciple. He even mentions a saying by Ka'b al-Ahbār, who maintained that the Prophet had in fact seen God *twice,* adding, with all the authority of an expert in Judaism (even though he contradicted the Bible in this particular case), that Moses had also spoken with God twice.[5] This reminds us once again of the old tripartite schema: Abraham—Moses—Muhammad. In fact, that schema was attributed, precisely, to Ibn 'Abbās. A vision is the most profound experience of the divine, and this vision of God is *fī ahsani sūratin,* as Ibn 'Abbās would have said, the vision of a benevolent and merciful God, very different from the terrifying aspect he would have at the Last Judgment.

But there were also conflicting traditions, resulting from a transcendentalist spirit that continues to this day. Consider Muhammad's wife 'Ā'isha who, in hadith, is frequently the interpreter of her husband's most personal experiences. 'Ā'isha emphatically denied that the Prophet had ever seen God. Elsewhere, we find compromises of every kind. It was said, for example, that the ascension, the vision, and the Prophet's night journey *(isrā')* had been only a dream: "He saw God" *(ra'ā Allāh),* but "he saw in his sleep" *(ra'ā fī nawmihī).* Some also claimed that Muhammad had not really seen God "with his eyes," but only *bi'l qalb,* "in his heart." In essence, that last explanation also amounted to a dream, a truthful dream. As it is said in the tradition, "the Prophet's eyes are sleeping, but his heart is not sleeping." The Koran taught that the soul returns to God during sleep, while the body remains in bed. In addition, the account of the vision ends with the sentence *mā kadhaba 'l-fu'ādu mā ra'ā,* "His heart did not lie about what he had seen."[6] Finally, there were efforts to dematerialize the object of the vision. Let us refer once more to a hadith. A certain 'Abdallāh b. Shaqīq al-'Uqaylī recounts: "I told Abū Dharr (al-Ghifārī): 'If I had met the Prophet, I would have asked him a question.' 'Which one?' 'I would have asked him whether he saw his Lord.' 'Well, I asked him exactly the same question.' 'And what did he reply?' 'He replied: "Light. How could I have seen him?"' [*nūr, annā arāhu*]."

The last sentence is somewhat difficult to interpret, and variants do exist. But the intention of the story is clear. Light has no form: thus, God does not assume any shape (*sūra*), and the vision is reduced to a sort of bedazzlement. In a sense, that was the philosopher's stone, a vision that did not interfere with transcendence.

Yet all these speculations also show that no one wanted to give up the vision as such; an angel was not enough. The staking out of that position was not at all an isolated or marginal phenomenon. We find evidence of it everywhere. I will limit myself to a single example, which might seem exotic but which mirrors the vast agreement buttressing the idea. In about AH 160, a strange figure, a "heretic," according to the Muslim sources, led a revolt against the Abbasid government in eastern Iran and Central Asia. This was the Muqanna‘, a man who veiled himself and to whom miracles were attributed; Jorge Luis Borges mentions him in one of his essays.[7] The Muqanna‘ believed that God embodied himself in the prophets—the first time in Adam when he created him *‘alā sūratihī*, in his image, and of course in Jesus as well, and finally in Muhammad. He is said to have entered Muhammad's body during the Prophet's vision, for at that moment he was "two bows' lengths or even closer," according to surat al-Najm. The heresiographical text regarding the Muqanna' himself, in which he revealed that he was an incarnation of God, renders this as "as close to him as an arrow is to its bow."[8] The scandalous aspect of his doctrine was precisely that idea of incarnation. To make it acceptable, the Muqanna' cited an exegesis of surat al-Najm that was clearly accepted by his audience. If he had invented it, he would not have been persuasive.

That leads directly to the second hypothesis. Muhammad saw God seated on his throne. That is a more difficult assertion to make, since it goes against not only the general view held by Muslims but also against the Western study of Islam. It is true that for philological reasons Orientalists generally assume that there is a vision of God in surat al-Najm, but they believe Muhammad saw God standing on the horizon. The Muqanna' was of a different opinion. The heresiographical passage I quoted says he believed that God returned to his throne after each manifestation or "incarnation." His conception of Muhammad's vision therefore implied that God had left the throne to draw near to the Prophet and to enter his body.

Once again, it is easy to quote other texts in support. But there is no need to do so, since we can refer to a witness who mentions the idea within the precise context of the *mi'rāj*. This is a hadith, a non-canonical and clearly apocryphal text that in its long version (about twenty pages) is mentioned only by al-Suyūtī in his *La'ālī al-masnū'a fī 'l-ahādīth al-mawdū'a*.[9] But al-Tabarī already quotes part of it, because the chain of transmission once more begins with Ibn 'Abbās.[10] He is followed by Dahhāk b. Muzāhim, a popular preacher *(qāss)* and exegete who continued the tradition of Ibn 'Abbās in Transoxiana. Dahhāk b. Muzāhim lived in Balkh, and it seems to have been from there that he transmitted the text in the region of ancient Bactria, where religions and civilizations had mingled and where a small Arab and Muslim community maintained commercial ties with Central Asia. Here are the essential lines:

> I looked toward him (God) with my heart until I knew he was truly there, that I was really seeing him *(hattā athbattuhū wa-athbattu ru'yatahū)*. And there he was, drawing back his veil and seated *(mustawī)* on his throne, in all his dignity and grandeur . . . In his majesty, he leaned slightly toward me and had me draw near [to him]. Such is his word in his Book, when he told you how he dealt with me and glorified me: ". . . one who is mighty and wise. He stood on the supreme

horizon; then, drawing near, he hung suspended
within two bows' length or even closer, and revealed to his servant that which he revealed,"
that is, the task he had decided to entrust
to me.

The task the text mentions is obviously the prophetic mission. There were some (Anas b. Mālik and
those who referred to him) who were even more precise: at that time, God revealed to Muhammad the
fifty prayers he wanted to impose on his community.
But Dahhāk b. Muzāhim placed the emphasis differently: on the vision of God. He did so cautiously. Muhammad had to close his eyes, and Gabriel himself
(who, of course, was very familiar with the effect of
that vision) covered his face with his hands. For an
instant, however, the Prophet was assaulted by the
full force of the light, and that is what he now saw in
his heart: God seated on his throne, drawing near to
touch him and to transfer his revelation in a truly
corporeal manner. "He placed one of his hands between my shoulder blades, and for a time I felt the
cool of his fingers touch my heart."

That leads to a third hypothesis. The vision of the
throne represents the starting point and the point of
reference in the theme of the ascension. If the Koran

seemed to confirm a vision of God seated on his throne, it was fairly easy to imagine that Muhammad had risen to heaven to see God on the throne. The new conception, however, included prominent and previously unmentioned features; suddenly there was the possibility of uniting the two visions into a single point of view. During his journey, Muhammad might have seen God first "on the supreme horizon," and then "near the Garden of Repose." In addition, the direction of the movement had changed. It was not God but the Prophet who had moved; and he was rising, not descending, as God or the angel did in the Koran. God never moves, he is immutable, according to a view established in antiquity and adopted soon thereafter by the transcendentalist theologians. He remains immutable in his majesty and receives the Prophet as a visitor, in an audience. But even the transcendentalists eventually overcame their distaste for the theme of the ascension. At the same time, it was now easier to salvage the Koranic passage on the *isrā'*. There again, it was the Prophet who moved, though horizontally, toward Jerusalem.

In principle, however, we need to distinguish between the night journey and the *mi'rāj*. Despite the fact that the two themes were melded together, they were fundamentally different. In Ibn Ishāq's biography of the Prophet, the two accounts are still separate. Ibn Saʿd even assigns them different dates. From the beginning, however, two things contributed to their being amalgamated. In the first place, the throne of God was said to be not only in heaven but also in Jerusalem. In that city stood his earthly throne, from which he had created the world and from which he would dispense justice at the end of time. And second, the night journey was sometimes understood as a rapture, a "mystical" translation to *al-bayt al-maʿmūr* of sura 52:4, the "Visited House," which people tended to see as the heavenly prototype for the Kaaba in Mecca and, as such, a "very distant place of veneration" *(masjid al-aqsā),* a heavenly Jerusalem, so to speak. That opened up a completely new dimension, which we cannot consider here. We are compelled to note, however, that as a result the accounts of the night journey sometimes also ended with a vision of God, and this vision was described in the same way as in the *miʿrāj*. The Prophet meets God in Jerusalem, in a garden of the *haram al-sharīf,* in a *hortus conclusus (hazīra)* as it was called—that is, within the walls surrounding the ancient Temple. It was there that Muhammad had seen God seated on his throne, in the form of a young man wearing a crown of light; and God touched him with his hand, between his shoulder blades, as a sign of friendship, and spoke to him.

Now that I have considered the history of the theme, let me conclude by attempting to establish a chronology. First, we need to emphasize that we have been dealing with exegesis and not reality. Whether the Prophet saw God or only an angel is a matter of faith; it cannot be resolved on the basis of texts. The Koran is clear in that regard in surat al-Takwīr, but not in surat al-Najm. The verses in surat al-Najm were certainly prior to those of surat al-Takwīr, but they do not seem to be the expression of an immediate experience simultaneous with the telling, for in that case the sura would not speak of two events and two visions at the same time. In addition, the text is homogeneous in appearance; the rhyme scheme is identical throughout the sura, with the exception of the six verses at the end (57–62). That is why we find no justification for the argument that the two visions were combined in a later revision, under 'Uthmān or earlier. Under such circumstances, we are compelled to hypothesize that the beginning of surat al-Najm does not describe a unique event that took place a moment earlier, but rather refers to two separate events, which by virtue of their singularity may have served to confirm the truth of something else. What, then, was the *Sitz im Leben* of surat al-Najm?

This topic remains to be examined. I cannot undertake a study of it here. Nevertheless, allow me to digress briefly again to al-Tabarī. In his *Tafsīr* and in his *Ta'rīkh,* he expresses fairly clear ideas on the question. According to him, what lies behind the very first part of surat al-Najm is the scandal of "Satanic verses."[11] The three pagan goddesses are mentioned in verses 19–20, immediately after the account of the second vision. The method they used to exert their influence, namely, intercession with Allah, *shafā'a,* is the theme of verse 26. Is the beginning of surat al-Najm, therefore, simply a speech, a sermon even, given by the Prophet when, as the accounts cited by al-Tabarī suggest, the Companions who had emigrated to Ethiopia returned to Mecca, ill informed about everything that had taken place in the meantime and desirous of knowing the Prophet's position on the rumors circulating? The Prophet, then, may have used all his authority and eloquence to defend himself against criticism. To do so, he evoked his encounters with the "numinous" (as we would now say). That is why the text says: "Your compatriot is not in error, nor is he mad! His is no language of passion. This is only revelation revealed to him. He is taught by one who is mighty and wise." The important thing was the encounter (or encounters) as such. In that regard, the question of whom he encountered was secondary. But the claim of having met God naturally carried more weight than that of having met Gabriel. For the moment, I cannot advance beyond that hypothesis; I am speaking of exegesis and not reality.

As far as the exegesis is concerned, we are faced with a totally different situation. The Koran had become scripture—that is, the canonized record of all the statements uttered by Muhammad as revelation. No one had forgotten that surat al-Najm might be somehow related to "Satanic verses." But this was no longer so important, for these verses were never incorporated into the final version of the Koran. The two visions of surat al-Najm were presented in a new light. Instead of being an allusion by the Prophet to a thing already known, to prove his truthfulness to an audience that may have briefly lost confidence in him, these visions were now understood as direct testimony of his encounter with the divine force. At the same time, the second Koranic reference to the event—namely, the statement from surat al-Takwīr—

began to exert its influence. When the Koran became scripture, a complete and unchangeable text, comparisons could be made, a network of references and cross-references created. At that point, theological reflection became a factor.

Under such circumstances, one can only be struck by how well accepted the anthropomorphic interpretation of surat al-Najm was in the early days of Islam, though we cannot be sure that the discussion on the subject actually goes back to the generation of the Companions. Much of what was said about the *Urgemeinde,* the early community, is derived from later projections rather than reality. Recent researchers have viewed Ibn 'Abbās as a sort of mythological figure.[12] As for the accounts attributed to 'Ā'isha, the supposition has been that she became aware of her husband's doubts concerning the interpretation of his visions. But her commentaries are mingled with polemical remarks against certain Shiite currents and are therefore apocryphal, or have at least been reformulated. As for the controversy as such, it is clear it did not begin before the end of the first century AH. During the caliphate of Hishām b. 'Abd al-Malik, between AH 105 and AH 120, Ja'd b. Dirham was executed in Iraq because, it was said, he denied that Abraham was the friend of God and that Moses had heard the voice of God on Sinai. He had apparently rejected the tripartite schema attributed to Ibn 'Abbās and, as a result, the vision of God accorded to Muhammad.[13]

It was also in Iraq that accounts of the *mi'rāj* seem initially to have spread. There, the idea of a heavenly journey was profoundly rooted in Hellenistic Gnosticism and in an apocalyptic and mystical form of Judaism. In Mecca and Medina, scholars proved cautious. Ibn Ishāq, who could hardly conceive of the idea that the Prophet had seen God in person, accepted only an attenuated variant of the account of the ascension. Syrians preferred to speak of a night journey; Jerusalem was the focus of their interest. They were not against the idea that Muhammad had seen God and had even been touched by him, but they did not see the need for an ascension. Nevertheless, the theme took root almost everywhere, probably because Iraq was, under the Abbasids, becoming the political and intellectual center of the Muslim world. From Iraq, the motif spread to Iran, where Iraqi troops had established themselves from the Umayyad caliphate onward. The longest text comes from Balkh. If it can legitimately be attributed to Dahhāk b. Muzāhim, it too was written in the first century AH.[14] Nevertheless, the first evidence of the theme as such that can be reliably dated comes from Iraq. Yet this account is unrelated to Muhammad. Its hero is a heretic who claimed to be a prophet himself: Abū Mansūr al-'Ijlī.

The figure Abū Mansūr is complex and difficult to interpret.[15] Suffice it to say that he belonged to the *ghulāt,* the lunatic fringe of ancient Shiism. He was executed on the order of Yūsuf b. 'Umar al-Thaqafī, governor of Iraq between AH 120 and 126, after rebelling against the Umayyad regime. To acquire legitimacy as a prophet, he claimed that he had been rapt up to heaven *('urija bihi ilā 'l-samā').* God is said to have invited him to draw near and to have spoken to him in Persian, calling him *yā pisar,* my son. He then sent Abū Mansūr back to earth with a mission to preach his word. Abū Mansūr seems thus to have considered himself the son of God; his followers called him Logos *(al-kalima)* and took oaths using that word. God had passed his hand over Abū Mansūr's head, and as a result Abū Mansūr called himself the Messiah *(al-masīh).* In Arabic, the word *masīh* signified something other than what it meant in the Aramaic language from which it was borrowed. The verb *masaha* did not originally mean "to anoint," as did *māshah* in Hebrew and *meshah* in Syriac. *Masīh* is not the "Christ," the Anointed, but "one over whose head the hand has been passed." Abū Mansūr's followers heard that word with Arabic ears. It was a very vivid way of appropriating the ancient theme. It seems that Abū Mansūr wanted to compete with Muhammad, but the model he followed was that of Jesus.

The important thing for us is that he failed, for the only thing his revolt accomplished was the occupation of a mosque. After that, no one could embrace with impunity the idea of ascension. Only a prophet could visit God. Meanwhile, the majority of Muslims came to agree that Muhammad had been the last prophet, the *khātam al-nabiyyīn*. In many respects, the Shiites disagreed with the majority view; for a time they held on to the earlier ideas. They also continued to embrace anthropomorphism, even after the era when prophets had arisen in their own community. But eventually they too changed their views and converted to the transcendentalism of the Sunnis. That change was due to a theological movement called Muʿtazila, whose systematic approach has determined Muslim thought even up to our own time. In the Mamluk era, when someone in Cairo claimed he had ascended to heaven and had seen and heard God, he was, after a jurist had been consulted, quite simply placed in an insane asylum. Conversely, the Prophet's *mi'rāj,* the founder's exaltation, had a long and glorious history in art and literature, even in a Latin text, *Liber Scalae Machometi.* In general, Muslims no longer accepted the idea that the Prophet had seen God; he had only heard his voice from behind a curtain. But they also no longer perceived the event as a mere dream. It was a real event, a miracle.

Nevertheless, the vision of God did not entirely lose its importance. The Sunnis engaged in long controversies over whether after the Last Judgment the *ru'ya bi'l-absār* (the "beatific vision" of the Christians) would be part of the joys of paradise, and finally they decided that such would be the case. All Muslims would see God in paradise—as if in a theater when the curtain rises—as a manifestation of divine grace. But by then the world would have reached its end, and the vision would be the apogee of eternal bliss. The Prophet, conversely, still had a task to carry out and for that reason returned to earth. His glorification marked the beginning and not the end. He became the symbol of Muslim identity, and in that respect his uniqueness was felt more than ever. But in our own time that uniqueness has been defined in the first place by the categories of the world here below, his role as lawmaker and spiritual guide. In the end, his supernatural encounter with God remained an isolated event. In that regard, Islamic thought, by comparison with Christian theology, has always respected the limits of the human condition. That may be an advantage.

3

THEOLOGY AND SCIENCE

Mu'tazilite Atomism

THERE IS SOMETHING very modern-sounding about the word "atomism."[1] But appearances can be deceiving. The Muslim theologians I wish to discuss were atomists, but their atomism was different from our own. Like the Greeks, they dealt with it in a purely speculative manner. However imaginative they may have been, they never felt the need to verify the existence of the atom; they simply posited it as a theoretical necessity. For them as for the Greeks, an atom was what the literal meaning of the word indicates: an indivisible entity, *juz' lā yatajazza'*. It did not occur to them to split it. They were not precursors, they were heirs. But as heirs, they displayed originality; their approach was unique. In that respect, they were modern in their own society and for their time in history.

Theirs was a complex inheritance. Several points of

view and models could be drawn from it. The Greek past was remote, but it was not entirely forgotten. People's brains were still filled with ancient notions and ancient problems. Despite the emergence of Islam (and before it of Christianity), the program for research—by which I mean the mental program, the human computer code, the categories of thought, and not the education system—had not changed a great deal. That was true in the Orient as well as in Constantinople and Rome. But in the place and time at issue, the Iraq of the Abbasids, traces of antiquity mingled with other influences: those of Sassanid Iran and even India (in medicine, for example, but also, famously, in arithmetic). So much freedom of choice soon brought trouble. Hence our first question: Why did Muslim theologians, *mutakallimūn* as they were called, opt for atomism?

Atomism was far from a passing hypothesis. The model had been used by a few pre-Socratic philosophers and revived and reinterpreted by Epicurus. Enormous resistance was mounted against it by Aristotle in his *Physics,* by the Stoics, and by the Neoplatonists. David Furley has spoken in this context of the cosmological crisis in classical antiquity; what he means by that is precisely the profound difference of opinion regarding the origin of the world and of things.[2] That difference was exacerbated by new axiomatic positions. Philosophers had been replaced by theologians. Henceforth, not only the world but God as well was in play. We could even wonder whether there was really a place for God within atomism, a system that, at least since the famous controversy between René Descartes and Pierre Gassendi, has represented the epitome of materialism. Nevertheless, the Stoics in their works include the chapter *Peri theōn*, "On the Gods," in the part on physics; theology and cosmology were never systematically separated. Even Aristotle's *Metaphysics*, the *ilāhiyyāt* of Arabic philosophers, did not initially go as far "beyond" *(meta)* physics as we think. It was not yet conceived of as something transcendent but was a subject addressed "after" the *Physics* in the curriculum of the Peripatetics' lyceum. But it might have been easier for a theologian to find inspiration in Aristotle's Unmoving Mover or in the One *(hen)* of the Neoplatonists. The Church Fathers decided to move in that direction. They despised atomism because they saw it as an attempt to explain the world in a wholly mechanical way, without metaphysical principles, simply as a result of chance, with no creation and no God. And they were wary of the Epicureans, whom they considered vulgar people who demonstrated their materialism through their lifestyle.

The most ancient Muslim theologians may have been of the same opinion. Some researchers have hypothesized that thinkers during the Umayyad caliphate, Jahm b. Safwān in Iran or Ja'd b. Dirham in Mesopotamia, for example, followed a Neoplatonist model that led to a profoundly apophatic theology, a theology of *tanzīh,* uniqueness, that was little concerned with the world. This was a "theology" in the true sense of the word, a logos about God *(theologia)* with no digressions into physics or cosmology.[3] Unfortunately, the few shreds of information that have come down to us are not enough to form a clear and unequivocal idea about them. But if that hypothesis is correct, we can imagine that Harran, in Upper Mesopotamia, capital of the last Umayyad caliph but also seat of a Neoplatonist school and bastion of a pagan astral religion, played a role in the transmission of these ideas. Ja'd b. Dirham lived in Harran, and Jahm b. Safwān may have studied there.[4] In any case, atomism was not present from the start in Muslim culture. Rather, it was discovered and developed at the apogee of the Abbasid dynasty by a generation that included Mu'ammar and Abū 'l-Hudhayl, who taught during the caliphates of Hārūn al-Rashīd and al-Ma'mūn. Shortly after they had constructed their new approach, the anti-atomist resistance coalesced once again. The form of Neoplatonism championed by al-Kindī and his team of Christian translators put the works of Plotinus and Proclus into circulation, evidently under the label "theology in the manner of Aristotle," that is, metaphysics.[5] The Christian theologians of the time who wrote in Arabic—'Ammār al-Basrī, Abū Rā'ita, Theodore Abū Qurra—also based their thinking on a Neoplatonist vision. The translators could thus feel they were being true to their own religious tradition. Conversely, the path the *mutakallimūn* were to take is much more difficult to discern. Mu'ammar and Abū 'l-Hudhayl had no translations to rely on. No text by Democritus or Epicurus was ever available in Arabic. And though the origins of the *Bayt al-Hikma,* or House of Wisdom (the famous library of the Abbasids), dated back to the caliphate of Harūn al-Rashīd, the translations it produced do not seem to have made an impression on the major figures of atomism. Abū 'l-Hudhayl and Mu'ammar were trained in Basra and not Baghdad, and they do not seem to have moved to the capital until al-Ma'mūn's reign.

*　　*　　*

Nevertheless, atomism did not come from nowhere, and its formation can be traced. Before Abū 'l-Hudhayl and Muʿammar, there was Dirār b. ʿAmr, a thinker from al-Kufa who visited Baghdad during the reign of the Barmakids. He was the first Muʿtazil-ite to develop a set of coherent notions about physics, and his approach was marked by the hypothesis that reality consists of parts that combine to form a body. That is the atomistic principle, but without the vo-cabulary normally associated with it, since the word Dirār uses to designate the "parts" *(baʿd)* is different from the word adopted for "atom" *(juzʾ).* And its meaning is also fundamentally different, for when he spoke of "parts," he was not thinking of particles or tiny bits of matter, but of phenomena by virtue of which any body whatsoever is perceived. He called these parts "accidents" *(aʿrād)* and described them as such: color and temperature, weight and state of the surface, animation or inertia, and so on. It is through these accident-parts that the body presents itself, and it is only in the form of these "accidents" that we can perceive it. Qualities exist only in combination; there is no color or temperature as such. But there is no substance either. The body is only a conglomeration of phenomena that form the parts of the image or the evidence we form of the body. The aim of that theory is less to explain reality than to describe our idea of it. Reality is what we perceive of it, a quantity of details that are all accidental but that, by combining, present themselves to us in the form of coherent objects. Richard Sorabji has spoken in this context of "bundle theory" and has found many examples of it in late antiquity.[6]

Abū 'l-Hudhayl seems to have been inspired by that model. He recognized its theological advantage: the "bundles" need someone to assemble them, and human beings can play that role only from the epistemological angle, as subjects of knowledge. If, however, one considers reality—that is, if one asks not only by whom the bundles are perceived but also by whom they are created—the answer can only be God. It is God who puts the parts together, and since real parts, not to say material parts, are now in question, it is better to use the term "atom." The phenomenological aspect has become secondary; for Abū 'l-Hudhayl, the "parts" Dirār spoke of are merely accidents that appear in general only after the fact. The atom, by contrast, is also a substance. God wills atom-substances to form bodies; that is called creation. To achieve the result he has in view—that is, to join together or assemble a quantity of atoms—God adds the accident of juncture, assemblage *(ta'līf);* he thereby creates dimension and corporeality. Naturally, he can also take away that accident of cohesion after some time; that is called disintegration, decomposition, death. And he can even add the accident of juncture a second time. That is what will happen at the resurrection, when God will bring human beings back to life and will create a new earth. He reassembles the bones, so to speak. But the metaphorical aspect of that image has now become obvious; the vision of Ezekiel, where that conception appears for the first time in the Old Testament, is replaced by a scientific construct.[7]

Atomism as *ancilla theologiae,* subject to the will of God, is what Abū 'l-Hudhayl wanted to achieve. He changed a materialist model into an instrument of monotheism, at first in a wholly speculative way, but in a manner perfectly consistent with Koranic revelation. He had satisfied the postulate of oneness, *tawhīd:* Everything that is made depends ultimately on God, except human free will. There is no nature in charge of things, and atoms, particles of being, do not act on their own or by chance. Fundamentally, they are only symbols of divine power. In fact, God does not even use them as building blocks. Rather, he calls things into being through his creating word, the *kun,* the "So be it" recorded in the Koran, and he does so all at once, without physical genesis.[8] On that matter, Dirār held the same view. But his approach was too sensualistic; his epistemology implied a concept of being that made the existence of God difficult to prove. In fact, it was Abū 'l-Hudhayl who formulated the first proof of the existence of God in Islam.[9] With what had originally been a materialist model, he overcame materialism. He was able to satisfy the requirements of his time.

The two distinctive elements in that development, epistemological sensualism and the hypothesis of the atom, indicate the likely site at which Muslims were able to revive that tradition: Iranian cosmology. Indeed, it is only in relation to that cosmology that Arabic sources mention these two elements as something living and contemporary. Christian theology does not breathe a word about them, either in Arabic or in Syriac; Greek philosophy was known only through literary allusions, and only imprecisely at that. Aristotle's *Physics* had not yet been translated, and the doctrines of the pre-Socratics were still unknown.[10] Although we have few accounts of Iranian cosmology, there is no doubt that the Muslims were very familiar with it, especially in Basra, where a large part of the population spoke Persian. Doxographers summarized it and theologians vigorously attacked it. Those against whom they directed their polemic were not phantoms; they lived in their region, and the two camps ran into each other in the homes of middle-class city dwellers.[11] People had taken to finding fault with the Manichaeans for their sensualism, that is, their belief that only what can be perceived by the senses actually exists. The criticism was false and was frequently used to demonstrate that those Muslims who were spiritual descendants of the Manichaeans—namely, the *zanādiqa,* learned men and intellectuals who did not directly reject the principles of Iranian cosmology—were not only heretics but also libertines. In relation to the earthly world, however, the remark was probably justified. The Manichaeans of that time—and along with them many other dualists—presented their religion in a scientific form without appealing to irrational convictions. They wanted to explain the world, and in that respect their sensualism or empiricism was shared by an entire generation of Muslim theologians. In addition to Dirār, for example, there was also his Basrian contemporary al-Asamm.[12] The principle remained valid so long as the concept of God was strictly apophatic; if God is the Other par excellence, he is beyond our reason just as he is beyond our senses. The world can be analyzed through phenomena, but God is accessible only through revelation. That view is still expressed by Dirār, but no longer by Abū 'l-Hudhayl.

The atomism defended by Abū 'l-Hudhayl was less characteristic of the Iranian tradition than was sensualism. The atomistic model appears there only as an option, and not even the first option. The key notion was rather that of mixture. In all the dualist systems known at the time, the two first principles, light and shadow, had to mix in order for the world to form. To separate that process from mythology, one had to invoke the traditional Stoic philosophical category of *krasis di' holou* rather than the atomism of Democritus and Epicurus. That was not 100 percent true, however; there were atomists among the *zanādiqa*, as the doxographical sources tell us.[13] The phenomenon they sought to explain with that approach was primarily motion.

The mechanics of motion had always attracted attention. For Aristotle, motion was one of the six kinds of change—namely, change in relation to place brought about through locomotion. There were other sorts of change—change in relation to substance, for example, which manifested itself in the phenomena of genera-

tion and corruption, or change in relation to accidents: a body gets hot after being cold, and so on.
For the dualists, these two sorts of change were explained by mixture. But motion was different, fleet-
ing and difficult to pin down. In contrast to material changes, the body in motion always remains the
same; the result of motion is manifested only in dis-
placement, after locomotion has ended. Aristotle had
interpreted motion as a coherent process; he thought
in continuist terms, as do we. But it was only a hypothesis, an axiom that was rather vague at the time
and difficult to prove. What happens during motion?
To make the problem more transparent, one can always imagine that the interval separating the beginning of the motion from the end of it is shortened to
such a point that a hypothetical body found somewhere at a given moment is found immediately after-
ward, "at the second moment" *(fī 'l-ḥāl al-thānī)*, in a
different place. Since only a minimal amount of time
has elapsed, the second place ought to be contiguous
with the first. And if, again in the interest of greater
clarity, one imagines that the moving body is also reduced to minimum size, one arrives at a model in
which atomic units move over a surface that consists
of compartments entirely occupied by these units.

Naturally, actually existing bodies consist of a quantity of these atoms and their motion is more reminiscent of the way a millipede walks. But one can imagine an ant or a mite instead. At every instant in its movement, it is faced with a contiguous compartment in a discrete space. In fact, the modern Arabic word for "atom" is *dharra,* which originally meant a small, undefined insect—a mite, if you like.

We do not know whether the dualists—or more precisely, those among them who were working from the atomistic hypothesis—understood the model in that way; the documentation is missing. But we are certain that Abū 'l-Hudhayl conceived things in those terms.[14] Even in his case, however, the sources are sparse: we have no original texts, only the accounts of doxographers. But Abū 'l-Hudhayl's view of things caused a great stir. The theory he advanced was repeated and discussed for centuries. In the fourth and fifth centuries AH, more than a century after his death, the theory was erected into a rigid scholastic system. For this period, texts abound, relatively speaking. The present difficulty stems from the fact that these texts have become available only recently; some have not been published yet, and the editions that do exist are far from reliable. We must always be wary of reconstructing a later period on such a basis. Up to now, no one has considered what happened during the phase separating Abū 'l-Hudhayl from his epigones.

For Abū 'l-Hudhayl himself, it is self-evident that every "substance," whether a body or a simple atom, is found somewhere; it occupies a concrete place. That is what he calls *kawn*, "location."[15] Alongside the *kawn*, there is the *makān*, the place that can be filled by an object, and the *mahall*, an accident's substratum. During motion, the object changes its *kawn*, but before arriving at its new location it can be found in several *amkina* (the plural of *makān*) or spatial points, points at which it does not pause and which remain devoid of its presence. Abū 'l-Hudhayl's set of axioms does not provide for eternal motion, a preclusive decision that, coming from a theologian, is readily understood. According to Abū 'l-Hudhayl, even the blessed will stop moving in paradise eventually, and the motion of the stars and spheres will cease with the end of the world.[16] In addition, the points—or rather the compartments—touched by an object as it moves are all of equal value. Nothing possesses a place proper to it and toward which it tends, an *idios topos,* as Aristotle would have said. Nevertheless, the compartment occupied by an atom is reserved for it thanks to the *kawn;* in no case could two atoms share the same place. That characteristic would later be called *tahayyuz,* the quality of filling a place.

For subsequent generations, that *tahayyuz* was an accident—the only accident, moreover, that was indispensable to the atom.[17] Conversely, Abū 'l-Hudhayl, who was unfamiliar with that term, conceived of the *kawn,* in which the *tahayyuz* was preformed, as it were, only as something indefinable but individual and perceptible—a *ma'nā,* it was called at the time. What interested him most was not the atom pure and simple but the *ta'līf,* the accident by virtue of which atoms form something coherent by joining together, that is, by filling two or several contiguous compartments at the same time. As a result, the problem of motion was raised in a different form. For a complex body, motion was an accident whose substratum was divisible, and the question arose whether that accident was inherent in all the atoms of the substratum or whether it occupied only a few of them. That question would soon be of great importance. For the moment, however, no one knew whether the system would have a chance to develop, since Abū 'l-Hudhayl found himself facing a criticism that went to the heart of the matter. It came from his nephew al-Nazzām and is the reason that the discussion for a while focused only on the principle—that is, on the possibility of proving the atomistic hypothesis pure and simple.

Al-Nazzām represents the other panel in the cosmological diptych that Islam inherited from antiquity. His network of axioms is anti-atomistic and is based rather on concepts formerly known and accepted by the Stoics. But once again, the resulting philosophy was filtered through the Iranian tradition. In addition, the cluster of categories he had received from the dualists was much clearer and broader in scope than it was for Abū 'l-Hudhayl. His governing idea was mixture, though he refrained from using that term too often. For him, bodies are not aggregates of atoms in which conflicting qualities alternate in the form of accidents. Rather, these qualities themselves are bodies that intermingle. An apple, for example, is a body that consists of other bodies, namely, color, odor, taste, and so on, which intermingle—"interpenetrate," as al-Nazzām said. There are simple bodies and mixed bodies, and the simple bodies (colors, tastes, and so on) are the aspects as which mixed bodies (the apple) present themselves. In a sense, the old sensualism was not yet forgotten, and Dirār's theory was once more on the ascendant. What had in the past been called "accidents" were simply replaced by "bodies." But alongside actualized and visible qualities, the mixed body also contains unperceived potential qualities. However hot an object may be, within it is always simultaneously a certain quantity of coldness; otherwise it would burn. Different qualities can alternate in a mixed body only because opposites are hidden inside. As soon as one of the opposites comes to the surface, the body changes in appearance. Nevertheless, it continues to exist as a coherent entity only by virtue of the balance of opposite qualities. If one of them abolished the other completely, the composite body would disintegrate (through being consumed by fire, for example). All the qualities thus exist simultaneously and, in a sense, in the same place as well. Similarly, all the qualities were created at the same time. It is God who put them together in a mixed body and who maintains their balance despite the fact that they are opposites. The only accident in this whole mixture is motion, but motion understood in the broadest sense of the word, as the principle of change.[18]

For al-Nazzām, motion in the restricted sense—that is, motion understood as locomotion—occurs in a continuous and infinitely divisible space. According to him, then, the moving object does not proceed from one compartment to another, and it is not always associated with a certain *makān*. Rather, it "jumps" from time to time, to cross infinity. The theory is both original and complicated; I shall not describe it in detail here.[19] But we must keep in mind the difference between the models. Al-Nazzām's continuous space is that of Euclid and Aristotle; by contrast, the atomists declare that space is discrete. It is possible that Abū 'l-Hudhayl had not yet clearly perceived the incompatibility between the two concepts; perhaps he had not completely realized that atomistic matter presupposes an atomistic space. Even a theologian such as Abū Hāshim, who lived more than a century later, did not accept that conclusion. In any case, al-Nazzām's merit was to have put his finger on the problem areas. These were not totally unknown: together, Abū 'l-Hudhayl and al-Nazzām sometimes repeated the commonplaces of an inherited philosophical discourse. Both, for example, tried to make use of Zeno's paradoxes, or what had become of them. But all this can hardly overshadow the fact that it was only at this moment that discussion began in Muslim theology and that a number of elements in that discussion were new. If the atom fills a compartment and touches others, it must have sides.

Why, then, wonders al-Nazzām, is it said that the atom acquires extension, length, and later width and depth only in contact with another, through juncture *(ta'līf)*? An entity that has sides will also always have dimensions.[20] And why would it not be possible to imagine an atom that stands at the juncture of two other underlying atoms? That superimposed atom would then "claim" both at once, but only halfway, which amounts to saying that the two would be divisible.[21] The arguments are problematic, even false; they show that al-Nazzām had trouble abstracting from sensory data and accepting the axioms of a noncontinuist geometry. Hence, he sometimes stops short of his conclusion. He constructs an interesting argument concerning the diagonal in a square, for example, but does not say that in a square the length of the diagonal is always an irrational number (the square root of 18, 32, 50, and so on), which can never be represented by discrete, atomistic units.[22] He was not a mathematician, and his capacity for abstraction was generally less well developed than his uncle's. But he forced the atomists to make their theory more explicit.

It appears that Abū 'l-Hudhayl assumed that all atoms are equal and homogeneous. They have neither hooks nor rings, by contrast with what Democritus had said; and as Epicurus suggested, they can appear in different forms. Mu'ammar, a contemporary and colleague of Abū 'l-Hudhayl, had imagined that eight of them form a cube, four on the bottom and four on the top. That is conceivable only if one assumes that every individual atom also presents itself in the form of a cube, a hexahedron.[23] Yet it would be a distortion to say that they are cubes, for a dimensional body, according to Mu'ammar, results only from eight atoms' being placed together. Two atoms form only a single dimension: length; and even when two others are added to them, the result is only length and width, without the depth necessary to any corporeal entity. Similarly, it would be unwise to propose that two atoms form a line, two lines a surface, and two surfaces a body; only dimensions are at issue. That reasoning becomes clear when it is compared with that of Abū 'l-Hudhayl, who claimed that six atoms were sufficient to form a body: two for the left and right, two more for the front and back, and finally two for the top and bottom. That never results in a geometrical body; even if one imagines a cluster, a coherent group without regular sides, a seventh atom would be needed in the middle. The six atoms mark only spatial directions.[24] In addition, the number of atoms was later reduced even further. Abū 'l-Qāsim al-Balkhī would say that four atoms suffice; one need only imagine that an unchanging central atom is paired with a second and that together they mark out left and right, then with a third to mark out front and back, and finally with a fourth marking top and bottom.[25]

In all these models, the atoms amount to "minima" *(elakhista)* understood in Epicurus's sense, but located in a discrete space that has the structure of a three-dimensional grid. They fill a compartment, and one can visualize that compartment as a square, like one on a chessboard. But as to their form, one must always keep in mind that the cube is only a metaphor. The atoms *resemble* cubes, as a later theologian said. To be real cubes, they must be bodies. They are not points; the term "point" is part of Euclid's continuist geometry. But we still need to resolve the question of whether they have extension. In his pioneering book published more than half a century ago, Shlomo Pines responded in the negative; in fact, we know of no text that provides a response where Abū 'l-Hudhayl is concerned.[26] There is no doubt, however, that fourth-century theorists replied in the affirmative, in invoking the category of *tahayyuz*. Abū 'l-Hudhayl had only *kawn*, "location," and he did not yet conceive of *kawn* as an accident. But though he had not yet clarified his categories, the internal dynamic of his system pushed it in the direction his successors were to pursue. These successors, haunted by al-Nazzām's objections, hastened to make that dynamic explicit.

But was the theory adequate to explain reality? Let us consider horses at a racetrack, for example: What happens at the atomic level? They run at different speeds and can accelerate. Perhaps the example is too complex; a motion executed by a living thing is also an action, and that adds a new dimension. Yet the same phenomena can be observed in an inanimate object—an arrow, for example. When an arrow moves after it is shot, it does so at a constantly decelerating speed. To explain its motion, one would have to introduce the factor of time. Abū 'l-Hudhayl does not seem to have thought of that. The doxographers did transmit his definition of time—which is a rare thing in the sources available to us—and he even developed it from an atomistic foundation, speaking of the instant *(waqt)* instead of continuous time *(zamān)*. But his intention is anthropological rather than physical; he seeks to explain the relation between time and human acts.[27] He also knew that motion always unfolds in time, proceeding from a first instant *(waqt awwal)* to a second *(waqt thānī)*. But in considering the phenomenon of acceleration and changing speed, he limited himself to an altogether material context. He said that motion as an accident is connected not simply to the compact body as a whole but to its particular atoms. It is not necessary for *every* atom of the body (of the arrow) to be occupied by a unit of motion; even if only some serve as a substratum for that accident, the concrete body begins to move or does not completely stop moving. The other atoms are occupied by units of pause, *waqafāt,* as Abū 'l-Hudhayl put it; the relation between units of motion *(harakāt)* and units of pause *(waqafāt)* determines the speed.[28]

Abū 'l-Hudhayl's system differs from Epicurus's in its details. Epicurus had explained the phenomenon of acceleration by the fact that at first the atoms of a moving body do not all move in the same direction. It is only after a certain time that motion becomes uniform. Every directed motion thus passes through a stage of inertia. Conversely, Abū 'l-Hudhayl tried to quantify the process. It seems, moreover, that his distinction between *harakāt* and *waqafāt* corresponded better to his concept of discrete geometry. All the same, his solution raised particular problems. It was necessary to take into consideration that in general the accident of motion is conferred on the moving object by an external force, often a human being. And sometimes the force is exerted by two people at once —if, for example, two people want to move a stone. We must then imagine that each of the two acts on only part of the atoms; the people divide them up between themselves, so to speak, each according to his or her individual strength. But let us suppose the atoms are odd in number; in that case, the two people could never apply their force equally.[29]

We do not know whether Abū 'l-Hudhayl would have been impressed by such an argument. He might still have said that for a slow-moving stone there are always atoms not yet occupied by an accident of motion. Since we do not know their number, we do not know whether that number is odd or even. The argument cited, in fact, was not directed against Abū 'l-Hudhayl but against one of his contemporaries, Bishr b. al-Muʿtamir. The concession the atomists would eventually make on that question was to maintain that even accidents—motion, but also color, and so on—are divisible. Something like accidental atoms exist, a consequence that corresponded poorly with the spirit of the system.[30] But that is no more than a detail. The most important thing is that once again al-Nazzām had considered the question. The difference lies simply in the fact that in his polemic it is always the theory of the "jump" that comes into play. He posited, for example, the dilemma of a man walking on a moving ship. In that case, the man is not going faster than the ship; nevertheless, he traverses a greater distance, for in the time it takes the ship to travel twenty yards, let us say, the man can advance from the stern to the bow—that is, another twenty yards. In relation to the surface of the water, he has thus traveled forty yards, whereas the ship has traveled only twenty. That has nothing to do with the number of atoms composing the man and the ship; he must therefore have jumped. We encounter the same difficulties in analyzing the process in relation to the surface of the water on which the two motions occurred. If we assume that the ship touched every compartment of that surface—and these compartments are atomistic by nature—the passenger must have touched only half of them while traveling twice the distance.[31] Let us take another example, a rotating millstone. The atoms move in concentric circles, and their number increases as these circles approach the periphery. Yet the distance traveled by the peripheral atoms during a complete rotation is much greater than that traveled by the atoms near the axis; they must therefore jump.[32]

The last theorem reminds us of another famous paradox known as Aristotle's Wheel, a problem discussed for the first time in Pseudo-Aristotle's *Mechanics*. Hero of Alexandria speaks of it as well. (It is interesting to note that his text survives only in Arabic translation.) In short, we are nearly certain that the roots of that whole multiform discussion go back to antiquity. Similarly, we find parallels to al-Nazzām's "jump" in the writings of the Neoplatonist Damascius and in other late Greek thinkers.[33] But the details of the argument are unknown to us, as are those of the generations immediately following the dispute, the theologians of the third century AH. Once again, we must resign ourselves to extrapolating from fourth- and fifth-century texts. Apart from a few remarks by doxographers, we have nothing precise on the first reactions to al-Nazzām's criticism. The later texts show us, however, that in the end the theoretical basis of atomism was refined and subtly modified. The difference in speed was no longer explained by the quantity of atoms occupied through an accident of motion. It was now said that motion could be interrupted by moments of pause or rest *(sakanāt),* infinitely small and imperceptible moments that cause the speed to abate.[34] In the millstone, for example, that is the case for the atoms located near the axis, by contrast with the peripheral atoms, which simply continue their course. These instants of rest were even observable on a cogwheel, more or less as they are on modern train station clocks or in a film when it is slowed down. By the end, the model, with that adjustment, had completely incorporated temporal atomism; the instants of rest could be conceived only as minima in Epicurus's sense. And the phenomenon of acceleration was now explained like any other motion, in relation to the underlying space and not in relation to the moving body. The theory had thus achieved greater coherence. The new hypothesis accepted the postulate of the usual model—namely, that an isolated atom (which can carry only a single accident of motion) advances, within one unit of time, only by a single compartment in space. Conversely, the explanation Abū 'l-Hudhayl had given could apply only in cases where there were at least two atoms. Al-Nazzām had certainly contributed toward clarifying the argument. But essentially, the dilemmas he had brought to light remained insoluble; at the level of axioms, the opposing parties did not speak the same language. Was it truly possible to posit that a millstone is composed merely of rings of atoms? It is a coherent object, and if at different points certain atoms pause, while others continue their course, the millstone shatters.[35]

Of course, atomism as conceived by Abū 'l-Hudhayl was not designed to be used by physicists. In fact, the little we know of the discussion by his earliest successors shows that at first it continued to focus on axioms. Abū 'l-Hudhayl's heirs were tremendously preoccupied by the relation between the atom and the body or—and this mattered a great deal to a theologian—by whether it is possible, in a fundamentally materialist model such as atomism, to distinguish between the inanimate world and living beings. The minds of the *mutakallimūn* were shaped by legal categories, and that is why they persisted in constructing a definition before solving a problem. As we have seen, they were constantly reducing the number of atoms necessary to form a body: eight, according to Muʿammar, six according to Abū 'l-Hudhayl, and finally, four for Abū 'l-Qāsim al-Balkhī. Hishām al-Fuwaṭī, one of Abū 'l-Hudhayl's disciples, had set out in the opposite direction, by postulating molecules with thirty-six atoms, but his idea met with no success. Some people were even ready to set more stringent limits: three atoms (Qalānisī), two, or even one.[36] Indeed, if one imagines a body in light of its definition, it is nothing but a composite *(al-mu'allaf)* formed by the *ta'līf,* the juncture or cohesion that holds its atoms together. And for a simple juncture, two atoms suffice. But the *ta'līf* is an accident; where, then, is its substratum? Can one really assume there is an accident inherent in two substrata at a time—that is, in the two atoms that have combined? Why not postulate that the *ta'līf* is located as a potentiality in each atom, while all the rest is only a verbal problem, given that one begins to *speak* of juncture only after it has actually come about? Atom and body would then be virtually identical, and it would be possible to forgo any discussion of the different connotations of the term *jawhar,* "substance."[37] The consequences were enormous for the general context of the theory. An atom that is joined only to a single other to form a body no longer needs sides; if the two touch, they become wholly indistinguishable. The man who defended that thesis, a certain Sālih Qubba, had studied with al-Nazzām; he knew that the idea of an atom with sides but no dimensions bordered on the absurd.[38] But he remained an atomist, for he postulated that every atom occupies a space and that two atoms occupy more space than one, despite the fact that the two are now found in the same place. His theory contradicts the evidence of the senses, but on the speculative level it was not lacking in coherence. Other people, though attacking its internal contradictions, embraced the basic approach. Al-Ash'arī himself believed that two atoms sufficed to form a body, and many Asha'rites followed him.

The second problem raised from the start belonged to what we would now call microbiology: the atomic structure of living beings. Nevertheless, as one might expect, the emphasis was placed on another dimension: anthropology. Dirār b. 'Amr had hypothesized merely that the human being, like any being open to perception, is composed of sensible and accidental phenomena that can be observed. In other words, one can perceive his warmth, his complexion, his smell. But his person is limited to that "bundle"; he has no soul, at least no soul independent of the body. The human being is reduced merely to the way he functions. His personality is manifest in his actions, which can be called good or bad in accordance with religious law. Dirār was a judge, and the categories he employed were not those of a philosopher. Nevertheless, it was some time before they came to be considered inadequate. True, Abū 'l-Hudhayl was quicker to realize that there was something that characterized the human being, beyond the bundle of phenomena that confronts us everywhere: there was also life. He thought about the human soul, and he may have seen the problem. But though the sources are even more imprecise here than usual, there is no doubt that he believed that the soul dies with the body. And when he found himself obliged to define the human being, he confined himself to such expressions as "the living body *(jasad)* that eats and drinks" or "the figure *(shakhs)* that has two hands and two feet."

The discovery of the immortal soul in Muslim theology is attributable to al-Nazzām (and in a sense to a Shiite theologian under whose influence he fell, Hishām b. al-Hakam). Al-Nazzām introduced the notion of *rūh,* or *pneuma,* which he included among the interpenetrating "bodies" that combine to form the human being. And he proved man's immortality with arguments Plato had developed in his *Phaedrus.* For him, life results from *pneuma,* and man and *pneuma* are, strictly speaking, identical. The body is no longer anything more than an envelope of flesh, corruptible and perishable, a *haykal,* a *Gehäuse.* The atomists, conversely, never found so clear a term to describe human singularity. They were convinced that the various parts of the human body do not act independently; rather, as they said, these form a totality, a specifically structured set *(jumla)* in relation to which life, knowledge, action, and so forth, present themselves as accidents or conditions—states *(ahwāl)*, to use Abū Hāshim's terminology. But fundamentally, the vocabulary remained inadequate because the system could not accommodate such complexity.[39]

Nevertheless, the majority of Muʿtazilite theologians turned away from al-Nazzām's ideas. This rejection is somewhat surprising, for from a modern perspective they were not without merit and can even be considered more advanced. But controversies once bore a different emphasis. Al-Nazzām did not provide a satisfying concept to explain creation. It seemed that the elements that, according to him, combine in existing objects had been created all at once and were subsequently simply hooked together indefinitely, as in a rail yard.[40] His theory of motion offered only one original idea, the "jump." But the fundamental axiom, that of motion as something continuous, could be demonstrated only after the invention of infinitesimal calculus by Pascal and Leibniz.[41] The *pneuma* hypothesis ran the risk of leading to the doctrine of a universal soul; in fact, certain disciples of al-Nazzām believed in metempsychosis.[42] Atomism, despite the problems specific to it, seemed to be the better alternative.

But at least in the long run, those who embraced it had to take into consideration the growth of philosophical and doxographical knowledge. Since the time of Ishāq b. Hunayn (d. AH 289), a translation of Aristotle's *Physics* had been available, and fragments of Epicurus's philosophy were known, in the Arabic version of Pseudo-Plutarch's *Placita philosophorum*. That additional information, a new burst of acculturation, so to speak, seems to have turned theology in the direction of physics, toward the real aspects of the theory. It was only then that people began to reflect that an atomistic world necessitates the existence of a vacuum. Abū 'l-Hudhayl had not mentioned its existence, nor had al-Nazzām. This is odd, for Democritus had raised the question from the outset. In fact, it is difficult to understand how atoms can move in a discrete space if no compartments are unoccupied. But the originality of the theologians had consisted precisely in separating atomism from the operation of this sublunary world. Where the Greeks had spoken of *physis,* nature, the theologians always spoke of God. Given that they already had a knowledge of Aristotle's thought—al-Nazzām claimed to have refuted it—they might have referred to the fact that Aristotle had seen no need to postulate anything like a vacuum. The Stoics had believed in the existence of a vacuum, but they imagined it only outside the universe. A few *mutakallimūn* thought that way as well. But a vacuum outside the universe has no importance for the theory of motion. A vacuum within the world is a more serious matter; why accept something nonexistent and incommensurable, in the order of the universe or in God's creation? Strato of Lampsacus had already demonstrated that if a stone is thrown into a receptacle filled with water, the stone merely changes places with the water. Instead of occupying an empty place, the stone puts itself in the place of another material. Abū 'l-Hudhayl seems to have assumed that where there is no object, space is filled with air. It is the air in a room that prevents the walls from moving together and joining. As Abū 'l-Hudhayl said, air is the place *(makān)* for bodies. In addition, he did not speak of the space in which a particular object is located, but of a place where it is found, and that place is only an accident of the object itself. It is in the same spirit that Abū 'l-Qāsim al-Balkhī began to do physics experiments similar to those done by Strato more than a millennium earlier.

It was precisely these experiments that excited curiosity and criticism. Abū Hāshim observed that it is impossible for animals to live in a deep well and explained that fact by the absence of air, that is, by a vacuum. Others were inspired by passages from the *Physics* in which Aristotle mentioned identical experiments, which he attributed to Anaxagoras. Hero of Alexandria also exerted an influence. Gradually, views changed. Qādī ʿAbd al-Jabbār, a Muʿtazilite master at the turn of the fifth century AH (eleventh century CE), considered the existence of a vacuum indispensable, and his disciple Abū Rashīd proved it, in opposition to the Baghdad "naturalists" *(ashāb al-tabāʾiʿ)*, an ambiguous term that seems to conceal nothing less than the Abū 'l-Qāsim al-Balkhī school, to which Abū Rashīd had previously belonged. The so-called Basrian school that he later joined managed to extend its influence beyond the Muʿtazilites, and the existence of a vacuum was accepted by the majority of the Ashʿarites.[43]

Atomistic theory had reached its apogee. In the following periods, its contours gradually blurred. We do not know when atomism died out. In the long run, the theologians, facing growing antipathy, tended to dispense with the preliminaries of physics. Simultaneously, the enormous success of Ibn Sīnā's philosophy offered an invitation to adopt a new infrastructure. Ibn Sīnā (Avicenna) did not like atomism; he refuted it in a long chapter of his *Physics*. Ultimately, he did not put much store in the *mutakallimūn*. In that respect, he saw no difference between al-Nazzām and his colleagues. Yet that general rejection was somewhat overstated; those who wanted to remain *mutakallimūn* continued to reflect on al-Nazzām's arguments. Fakhr al-Dīn al-Rāzī, though a good commentator on Ibn Sīnā, enumerated them all, only to refute them later in one of his philosophical works, the *Mabāhith al-mashriqiyya*. Al-Bīrūnī, a contemporary of Ibn Sīnā—he was seven years his senior—proved even more skeptical toward the new wave. He was familiar with Indian atomism and wondered somewhat caustically, in his famous correspondence with his young colleague, why Aristotle had treated the atomists so superciliously. Even in the Mongol period, certain theologians still followed the old system; the Shiite Maytham b. ʿAlī al-Bahrānī is a good example.[44] That is why the old ideas were still visible in a different garb. Bahā' ul-dīn Valad, father of Jalāl ul-Dīn al-Rūmī (Rumi), used atomistic concepts to convey his mystical psychology.[45] It is undeniable that the model developed by Abū 'l-Hudhayl was much more resistant to the passage of time than the systems that exist today. I am not altogether sure that that is a merit; but for what it is worth, the fact deserves at least to be pointed out.

4

THEOLOGY AND HUMAN REALITY

Historical Images and Political Ideas

BOTH THE REFORMIST and the fundamentalist currents of modern Islam take their inspiration from a vision of history that favors the beginning over the end, the past over the future.[1] Such a view unquestionably posits a utopia of the ideal beginning, so to speak. That sort of backward-looking utopian thought is fairly common. In nineteenth-century Europe, it took the form of nationalism; there too, a mythical past was constructed in an effort to forge an identity, and that mythical past was reconstituted through a slanted reading of the historical texts. We know, in fact, that utopias are never completely alien to reality. The problem stems from the fact that reality is violated by the interpretation imposed by the utopian view. For Muslims, a further element has been added—namely, revelation, which marks the beginning of historical reality and therefore forms an indelible part of the utopia. The divine message has been adapted with unexpected success to the contingencies of this world. It is perfectly logical to apprehend the Prophet as the founder of his community, who in his capacity as lawmaker created a new society. And it goes without saying that one can infer from this understanding the imperative to rebuild today's society in accordance with categories developed at the time. But it must also be recognized that that is not the only way to interpret the Prophet's role. True, the early generations of Islam knew, just as we do, that the new revelation had brought about a fundamental change. Compared with the pre-Islamic period, the *jāhiliyya,* Islam marked a radical turning point. But the Prophet was considered a spiritual guide above all, the model of perfect behavior at the ritual and moral level. That was the main content of the sunna. In the political realm at the time, it was instead the first caliphs who staked out the future, through their military campaigns beyond the Arabian Peninsula and their victories over the two great empires of the Old World, but also through their internal quarrels, the schism of the first civil war. It was then that the community definitively distanced itself from eschatological ideas and exchanged the ideal of

Bedouin freedom for the concept of a structured government—a "state," if you like.

In principle, the era of the Prophet's successors occupied center stage, historically speaking: no one was looking backward just yet. The feeling that something had been lost, that a break had occurred marking the end of an ideal era, a golden age, so to speak, developed only gradually and eventually took shape with the concept of the "rightly guided" caliphs, *al-khulafā' al-rāshidūn*. That concept was reinforced by the canonical number four. It did not appear for a long time—not before the first half of the third century, when Ahmad b. Hanbal was one of the first to defend it, and even then only at the end of his life. Why four, precisely, and not two or three? The Shiites never accepted that construct. One's view of history is always selective; it contains a certain element of arbitrariness. Therefore, we cannot refrain from asking: What else could have been incorporated into this view of history, and why was the exemplary reality we find in books (and, alas, only in books) finally decided on? Three of the first four caliphs were assassinated, so the reality was hardly as idyllic as the schema supposed. But these murders were nearly forgotten, with the exception, perhaps, of 'Uthmān's. As for 'Umar's, Muslims exonerated themselves on the pretext he had been killed by a non-Muslim and had thus died a martyr. The same was true for 'Alī: although it was not an unbeliever who had murdered him, it was surely a heretic, a Khārijite.

'Uthmān, by contrast, had been killed by true believers. In addition, his successor, 'Alī, was suspected of having had a hand in the affair, or at the very least of having benefited from it. In the long run, it was not the murder as such that was so shocking, but the resulting schism. The unity of the community collapsed; henceforth, there were the followers of 'Uthmān, the future Sunnis, and the followers of 'Alī, the future Shiites. Theoretically, it should not have happened that way, for division, in the Koran, was imputed to infidels, especially Christians. They had destroyed one another through their theological disputes. Islam, conversely, had reconstituted the primordial revelation. That development was a sign of divine mercy, said the Koran. Why, then, was there discord in the Muslim ranks, why were there division and bloodshed that would be perpetuated in the generations to come? God's commandment had clearly been broken, and the guilty party had to be found. People tried to justify themselves, or they blamed themselves; and so historiography came into being.

They wondered how good Muslims ought to have acted, and so political theory began. They constantly evaluated events by religious criteria, and so theology entered the picture. They spoke not of misconduct but of sin, and, as it happened, those who had killed one another were the Companions of the Prophet, and as a result the very ones who would become models for later generations.

Such is the constellation I would like to take as my starting point: the explosive mixture of historiography, theology, and political thought. The chronology is especially important. These three dimensions appear at the same time, and so early that they are part of the search for identity that was a driving force in the early generations and continues to be so today. That explains the efficacy of these ideas, and why people are still reinterpreting that past and rereading the texts that refer to it. These repeated rereadings also determined the fate of the sources available to us. Many interpretations soon lost their value, and when they were no longer in fashion, the texts in which they had been expressed no longer got copied. The loss was enormous. In the field of historiography we sometimes have the opportunity to reconstruct a lost work; for political theory, we have only doxography.[2] The summaries we find are brief and inadequate, and a great deal of imagination must be marshaled to restore their original plasticity.

The schism has continued into our own time. Ecumenical efforts began very early, but they all failed. Nevertheless, they influenced the shape of history and in turn produced schools of thought, sects, as they are generally called, alongside the two major faiths. Those who wanted to reconcile the camps were all of the opinion that it was no longer possible to impute the sin to a single guilty party or to a single group. In one way or another, they wanted to forget the whole affair. As a consequence, the Murji'ites, or "postponers," ultimately recommended deferring judgment; hence the origin of their name. At first, the doctrine of *irjā'*, postponement, was formulated in relation to 'Alī and 'Uthmān. The Murji'ites emphasized that no one knew any longer which of the two had committed the "sin." Initially, then, that view was a call for political moderation.[3] Later, when even the Murji'ite current was no longer in a position to remain neutral, the political principle was transformed into a theological doctrine: No one must call the faith of a coreligionist into question. God alone would decide who would be punished and who would escape punishment. In this world, all Muslims remain united by Islam.[4]

That position, which dates from the last quarter of the first century AH, integrated the lesson of the first two civil wars. Muslims were weary and hoped to re-establish peace by declaring a general amnesty. What followed was the opposite, a third *fitna*, fiercer and more widespread than the two previous ones. It culminated in the Abbasid revolution. In the climate of general confusion that reigned during the last decade before the advent of the new dynasty, a new group of theologians arose and tackled the same problem, though in a much more disillusioned manner. These were the Mu'tazilites. They addressed the contemporary situation, but spoke of it only indirectly. Instead, they evoked the earlier era—on which the Murji'ites had already taken a position—except that now they emphasized the dimension of sin much more strongly than the Murji'ites had. Sin had destroyed the *'adala*, that is, the integrity and reliability of those responsible for the battles during the first civil war. As witnesses, therefore, all of them were compromised. But since we do not know which of them was wrong, the situation resembled a case of adultery in which the partners engage in mutual repudiation *(li'ān)*. The marriage is voided, but the question of guilt remains unresolved. The testimony of both partners continues to be accepted, except when they testify against each other. The argument had thus taken a legal turn, which is characteristic of the *kalām* in general and is not as surprising as one might think. Nevertheless, we might wonder why they were so preoccupied with the testimony of people who had died two or three generations earlier. It was because they were thinking of hadith they had transmitted. It was by reference to those traditions that the schism was usually justified and reinforced. The *'adāla* in question is thus integrity as conceived by specialists in hadith.[5]

In a sense, the *ashāb al-hadīth* learned their lesson. They developed criteria to exclude overly one-sided traditions. But they applied these criteria only to others, "heretics." Among themselves, they did not manage to differentiate hadith from historiography. What emerged was the concept of the four "rightly guided" caliphs, in which the *'adāla* of the first ca-liphs was almost frozen. In the long run, even the Mu'tazilites embraced the concept. At first, only three caliphs from the first generation were recog-nized, and in fact it was not always the same three: Abū Bakr, 'Umar, and 'Uthmān in Medina and Basra, but Abū Bakr, 'Umar, and 'Alī in al-Kufa. In the late second century AH, a few *muhaddithūn* from al-Kufa made a concession, accepting Abū Bakr, 'Umar, 'Alī, and with some reservation 'Uthmān. After all, 'Uthmān had been one of the Companions *(sahāba)* or, more precisely, one of the *'ashara al-mubashshara,* the ten the Prophet had promised would go to paradise. Other *muhaddithūn* then felt impelled to reestablish the historical sequence—that is, to reverse the places of 'Alī and 'Uthmān, in privileging 'Uthmān and finally elevating him to the same rank as the others. The glorification of the four *khulafā' rāshidūn* had thus begun; it coincided with the canonization of the Companions.[6]

But what are we to make of the Battle of the Camel and the Battle of Siffin? After all, those who fought during these crises were Companions. A resolution was made claiming that those responsible for the murder of 'Uthmān and for the battles that followed were not the most highly regarded Companions, but people on a lower plane, Bedouins or Shiite extremists, who were called the *Saba'iyya* at the time. Sayf b. 'Umar was one of those who propagated that historical myth.[7] But the man who made it a truly scientific doctrine was the Mu'tazilite Hishām al-Fuwatī, a disciple of Abū 'l-Hudhayl who lived during al-

Ma'mūn's reign. For him, the Battle of the Camel was only a misunderstanding, a disaster caused by certain unreliable elements and not by protagonists such as Talha or Zubayr.[8] It is possible that Hishām al-Fuwatī was the sort of man who closed his eyes to reality. But the *ashāb al-hadīth* also began to favor a solution of that kind. Walīd b. Abān al-Karābīsī, a theologian from the Iraqi town of Wāsit who was a contemporary of Hishām al-Fuwatī but not a Mu'tazilite, thought that 'Alī and his opponents, in joining the battle, were only obeying their *ijtihād,* their independent reasoning. And in the *ijtihād* there is always room for an error that goes unpunished because *kull mujtahid musīb:* Whoever forms a reasoned opinion is right.[9] That legal variant was later accepted, albeit with a few modifications, by many theologians from the school of Ibn Kullāb and al-Ash'arī, Shāfi'ites especially, but also by Mālikites such as al-Bāqillānī.[10] There was a universal need to put the past to rest.

Hishām al-Fuwatī's position was certainly ideological. To shore it up, it was necessary to manipulate the sources, but the position had the advantage of neutralizing a discussion that had become fruitless. Hence, people could turn their attention to other subjects, to questions dealing with process pure and simple—succession, for example, or the political system as such. There were many problems to settle: Who would become caliph? Should he be elected, and if so, by what means? Could the power conferred on him later be taken away—could a caliph be deposed? Was government power, the state, an absolute necessity after all? Al-Māwardī was by no means the first to provide answers to these questions. From the beginning, theologians and jurists debated them at length.

As always and everywhere, however, care was taken to differentiate between theory and practice. Theory develops freely and takes its time; it usually comes fairly late. Practice has to be decisive; it creates realities. On the question of taking power, the practice of the "rightly guided" caliphs was far from uniform. Abū Bakr had been named by acclamation, but that acclamation was not planned in advance, it was arranged somewhat unexpectedly—*faltatān*, as 'Umar later declared: without a regular procedure. As for 'Umar, he was designated by his predecessor; he thus owed his power to Abū Bakr's will. 'Uthmān was elected by a council, a six-person *shūrā*, not by the people, as is sometimes now said, but by an electoral committee of which he was a member. 'Alī's position

as caliph was approved by the *bay'a,* the oath of allegiance taken by community leaders, except that, in
his case, that act of allegiance was not unanimous.
One entire group had backed out of it. He and his
followers did not attach a great deal of importance
to that. They believed that power belonged to the
Prophet's family and that those who did not bow to
it were simply wrong. Fundamentally, those who were
their enemies and who defeated them, the Umayyads
and the Abbasids, were of the same opinion: as much
as possible, they kept power within their own fami-
lies. They all shared the conviction that power was inherited or given by God. For them, election was not
an act, but an innate quality.

For 'Alī's followers, the future Shiites, that would
soon become pure theory. After 'Alī was assassinated,
they did not regain power until the advent of the
Fatimids in North Africa and later in Egypt. In real
terms, the major problem confronting their model
was that 'Alī had many descendants. Rifts among
the different branches were almost inevitable and in
fact occurred immediately. In theoretical terms, their
model collided with the fact that 'Alī had not been
the first caliph, but the fourth. His followers, since
they could not change history, changed the perception of it, the *Geschichtsbild,* to use the German expres-

sion. From that standpoint, 'Uthmān's case was clear: According to them, he was a good-for-nothing. But how were they to judge Abū Bakr and 'Umar? The Shiites began to write treatises about the day Abū Bakr was named caliph, *yawm al-saqīfa*, and they wondered how someone like him, who had no claim to the caliphate, could have been legitimately elected. The diversity of opinion was great, ranging from those who considered the election an excusable error to those who saw it as the result of a conspiracy. At one point, the theologians introduced a distinction between the rule of the "righteous" man, that is, the one most fit to govern because of his personal merit, *imāmat al-fāḍil*, and the rule of the man of inferior merit, *imāmat al-mafḍul*, who had nevertheless been elected by a majority. As always, the schema was applied only to the exemplary past, the classical age of the first caliphs. Abū Bakr was of lesser merit, *mafḍūl*, but he still had the right to be caliph. Seen in that light, the schema already had a Shiite bias: Abū Bakr was of lesser quality, inferior in merit, compared to 'Alī. The two terms may have been developed by the Mu'tazilites, but those among them who used the terms, Bishr b. al-Mu'tamir for example, belonged to the Zaydī current, which in this case means moderate Shiites who accepted the government of the

Abbasids.[11] Presented in that way, the schema can be seen as the product of a compromise.

As is only natural, opposition came from both parties to the compromise. It came first from those who considered Abū Bakr the preeminent caliph. They were in Basra, a city that had always supported 'Uthmān. But it would also come from Shiite extremists who completely rejected Abū Bakr, and 'Umar along with him. For them, both those caliphs, like 'Uthmān, had been usurpers. That idea was especially widespread in al-Kufa; those who embraced it were called the *rawāfiḍ*.[12] At first, they were merely one group among others. But they soon came to represent the majority, and their attitude was adopted by those who began to be called Imamis *(Imāmiyya),* or later Twelvers *(Ithnā 'ashariyya).* As the theologians argued over the respective qualifications of the candidates, they compared them with one another. To establish criteria, they developed catalogues of virtues. It was then that for the first time they spoke of the qualities necessary or desirable in a ruler. That is what Bishr b. al-Mu'tamir did, for example, introducing a theme that would be developed later by such Sunni authors as al-Māwardī. The Rāfidites took a different path; they did not like shades of gray. For them, it was not a matter of combining qualities, of whatever kind. If the power to rule—the imamate as it was called at the time—was passed down through a last will and testament or statement *(nass)*, the candidate's qualifications were secondary. In addition, there was no reason to consider the Companions of the Prophet examples of excellence. From the Rāfidite perspective, they were, with rare exceptions, all discredited by the fact that they had collaborated in the plot that allowed Abū Bakr and 'Umar, who were not part of the Prophet's family, to assume power at 'Alī's expense. Truth was not a monopoly held by the majority; the Shiites never accepted the principle of *ijmā'* practiced by the Sunnis.

What the Rāfidites had was only a theory of refusal. But there were other resistance movements that had nothing to do with the Shiites. They had their own ideology, based on different arguments. They relied on the Koran much more than the Shiites did. They liked to lay claim to the "Book of God and of His Prophet's sunna," and what that motto expressed was their desire to bring true Islam into being. They had a tendency to identify their propaganda with the obligation to command the good and to forbid evil,

al-amr bi'l-ma'rūf wa'l-nahy 'an al-munkar, a principle
also taken from the Koran. That was naturally all a
matter of exegesis; the obligation to command the
good lent itself to different interpretations. The
Mu'tazilites, for example, appropriated the motto in
their formative phase, when they were still in a position to oppose the government. Later, when they
were admitted to the courts of the Abbasid caliphs,
they hastened to give it a different meaning. Indeed,
the government also had an interest in "command-
ing the good and forbidding evil," and in doing so in
a way consistent with the Book of God and of his
Prophet's sunna. The problem had a long history.
Traces can already be found in hadith of a discussion
by scholars on that subject. How does one command
the good? By the sword *(bi'l-sayf),* by exhortation *(bi'l-
lisān),* or simply by internal disapproval *(bi'l-qalb)*?
Who has the right to act, and what action should be
performed? The responses varied, but they date from
as early as the Umayyad dynasty.[13]

When Muslims did take up arms, a verse from the
Koran entered the picture, shifting the focus. It is
surat al-Hujurāt 9: "If two parties of believers take up
arms the one against the other, make peace between
them. If either of them commits aggression against

the other, fight against the aggressors till they submit to God's judgment. When they submit, make peace between them in equity and justice." Of course, it was not always possible to know which was the *fi'a al-bāghiya,* the aggressor or rebellious party; regardless, the verse recommended reconciliation, resolution of the conflict, and not the militant pursuit of confrontation until the brutal outcome. Revolt therefore remained an irregularity, an exception, which the whole community had a duty to prevent. Even rebels who thought they were fighting for a just cause were in the wrong if they did not agree to negotiate or if the other party, generally the government, seemed to be making concessions. The discussion was broached with the 'Ali case. As a legitimate caliph, he had been able to treat his adversaries at the Battle of the Camel as a dissident group, the *fi'a al-bāghiya.* In Siffin, he again had right on his side. According to a well-known hadith, the Prophet had predicted to 'Ammār b. Yāsir that he would be killed by the *fi'a al-bāghiya,* that is, by Mu'āwiya's troops. But 'Ali had also agreed to arbitration, so that peace could be reestablished. The peace that followed was not altogether the peace he had wanted, and it was ultimately Mu'āwiya who prevailed. Nevertheless, the majority view was that 'Alī had made a good decision. In the long run, his religious prestige was greater than Mu'āwiya's, even among the Sunnis.

For theological discussion, the *bughāt* (rebels) par excellence were the Khārijites. They too had been repressed by 'Alī, but they had revolted again after his death and had sown terror with fanaticism and brutality. In the eyes of the middle class in Iraqi cities, they were extremists that the government was right to combat. The line between resistance and terrorism was increasingly blurred. Al-Asamm, a second-century Basrian Mu'tazilite, taught, moreover, that the ruler could not demand his subjects' loyalty against the *ahl al-baghy* unless he himself was "just"; the *ahl al-baghy* could be opposed only by the *ahl al-'adl*. After all, the verse in surat al-Hujurāt ends with the sentence "Make peace between them in equity and justice; God loves those who exercise justice" ("fa-aslihū baynahumā bi'l-'adl wa-aqsitū. Inna llāha yuhibbu 'l-muqsitīna," 49:9). But in the *Fiqh absat*, a Murji'ite treatise written by an Iranian Hanafite jurist in Balkh, the dilemma was settled in a completely different way. Subjects were obliged to persevere in their loyalty toward the government, even when that government committed injustices against the *ahl al-baghy*. 'Abdallāh b. al-Mubārak (d. 797) defined the *ahl al-sunna*—he was one of the first to use the term in a technical sense—as those who rejected insurrection in all cases and who prayed behind the caliph's representative, whether or not he was devout. Jurists were no longer concerned with the question of which was the *fi'a al-bāghiya* in a particular case; the *bughāt* were simply the rebels. The government had the monopoly on power.

All this means in essence that the theoretical basis of a right to resistance was rather weak. Of course, there was the hadith "No obedience to a created being with respect to sin!" *(lā tā'ata li-makhlūqin fi ma'siyati 'l-khāliq)*. But in his *Risāla fi 'l-sahāba,* Ibn al-Muqaffa' had already warned the caliph against a false exegesis of it. The Qadarites had used that saying of the Prophet; their propaganda had made it a fixed part of collective memory. Indeed, the Umayyads had claimed that their governmental power had been a gift of God, a *rizq,* predetermined and irreversible, and the Qadarites had protested, saying that power was worthless as long as one did not prove worthy of it. Their attitude was noble and justifiable, but it was linked to the heresy of free will. Even the militant fundamentalists of our own time prefer to define their resistance against the state as a resistance against the infidel. For them, it is not an intracommunity rebellion, a rebellion of Muslims against other Muslims, but a war, a jihad against the *kuffār*, infidels merely claiming to be Muslims. One does not make war against one's coreligionists.[14]

Yet power came ultimately from God and not from the ruler. The Koran had not singled out the Prophet as head of the community; God had addressed believers as such through him. For a century, minted coins, the most visible symbol of power, did not bear the caliph's name. Until the reign of the Abbasid caliph al-Mahdī, only religious mottos appeared on them. Poets did tend to address the caliphs as *khalīfat Allāh,* "vicar of God"; but theologians generally emphasized that he was only the *khalīfat rasūl Allāh,* the Prophet's successor when it came to earthly authority. It was the overarching importance of the community that led Sunni theologians and jurists, including many Mu'tazilites, to recommend the elective model even though the political reality did not directly favor it.

One might think that they debated about the consultation, the *shūrā,* a great deal in that context. But such is not the case; we must not be misled by modern concerns. Of course, the principle of the *shūrā* continued to play a role, but only under certain conditions. The *shūrā* was not an "election" but a "con-

sultation." Taken in that sense, the term could even
become a revolutionary postulate. The opponents of
Walīd b. Yazīd—that is, the Qadarites who supported
Yazīd b. al-Walīd—had used the term to justify their
cause, and Jahm b. Safwān, the Iranian theologian,
had used it at the end of the Umayyad dynasty to attack Nasr b. Sayyār, governor of Hishām b. 'Abd al-
Malik.[15] All of them, in fact, wanted not only to par-
ticipate in the exercise of power but actually to hold
power. Although mentioned in the Koran, the *shūrā*
does not trace its origin to the sacred text; it was
rather a legacy of tribal society and was always practiced oligarchically. For that reason, the Mu'tazilite
al-Asamm, who had on the whole a great deal of sympathy for the way the procedure had been applied by
'Umar, did not find it satisfactory in his own time.
This was under the Abbasids, and he demanded instead the unanimous agreement of all Muslims, a
true *ijmā'*, to warrant the naming of a caliph.[16] We
are not sure he believed that such an *ijmā'* had been
achieved in his time. But we know he believed that
unanimous agreement, once established, was irrevo-
cable. The *shūrā*, by contrast, could on principle always be replaced by another consultation. In his en-
thronement speech, Yazīd b. al-Walīd promised the
Damascene Qadarites who had elected him that he

would resign if they no longer found him satisfactory.[17] Fortunately, he died before that situation arose. But with his caliphate the third civil war began, leading to the Abbasid revolution.

The Abbasids drew the necessary conclusion. The concession made by Yazīd b. al-Walīd was never mentioned by them. Al-Asamm, who formulated his doctrine during the reign of Hārūn al-Rashīd, had to argue in an altogether different context, for the first Abbasids used a Shiite vocabulary to define their legitimacy. That is not surprising if we recall that it was the alliance with the Shiites that facilitated their revolution and guaranteed its success. Like the Shiites, they thought in terms of succession and felt they were legitimate heirs because, like them, they were *ahl al-bayt*, people of the house (that is, of the family of the Prophet). They even had an advantage over 'Alī; 'Abbās had been the Prophet's uncle, whereas 'Alī owed his legitimacy to his wife. That particularity was convenient for them when the alliance was broken, with the insurrection of al-Nafs al-Zakiyya under al-Mansūr. They could then claim that, according to divine law, when there was no son, the uncle had a greater right to the inheritance than the daughter. Legally speaking, it was an ingenious theory; the Shiites had some difficulty refuting it and as a result ultimately changed their entire legal system, giving women many more advantages in their law of succession than the Sunnis did. In spite of that, the Abbasids abandoned the theory fairly early, under Hārūn al-Rashīd. The advent of the Barmakids led to a change of strategy. The Shiites had been defeated on the battlefield and no longer constituted an immediate danger. Given that situation, reasons of state dictated a rapprochement with the Sunnis, the majority of the population not only in Iraq but everywhere in the empire. The jurists were thus free to return to the elective model. But in accordance with their logic, they continued to understand election primarily as a quality and not as an act. Instead of asking who was going to elect the caliph, they wondered which of the candidates was eligible.

The majority said: "They are of the Quraysh tribe" ("al-a'imma min Quraysh").[18] Abū Yūsuf held that view. He was the most eminent jurist in the court of Hārūn al-Rashīd, the first supreme judge, *qādī 'l-qudāt*, known to us. In supporting that thesis (he was not its author), he limited the number of candidates but did so realistically. The postulate that granted the Quraysh the privilege of being the only Arabs to assume power may already have been used in naming Abū Bakr. In fact, all the caliphs, both the Umayyads and the Abbasids, belonged to that tribe. But there was also a minority opinion formulated by a contemporary of Abū Yūsuf—namely, Dirār b. ʿAmr, the Muʿtazilite theologian mentioned earlier, who was himself a practicing jurist. He was a *qāḍī* not at the court or in the capital but in al-Kufa, and as a result among a population that was far from favorable toward the government. The objection formulated by Dirār against the privilege of the Quraysh was based on the observation that if irregularities or complaints arose, it was difficult to depose a member of a powerful clan. In saying that, Dirār was thinking of ʿUthmān and the protests directed against him because of his *aḥdāth,* his "innovations." If one is to avoid civil war, it is better to have a ruler who does not come from an influential family. Fundamentally, an Arab had no more right to the caliphate than a *Nabaṭī,* that is, a peasant from the Iraqi countryside who spoke Aramaic and did nothing but plow his fields and pay his taxes.[19] Of course, no one seriously thought of installing a Nabataean caliph. That was obviously a utopian idea. But Dirār was not wholly isolated; his idea was adopted by Thumāma b. Ashras, and later even by al-Jāhiz. He had predecessors: the Iraqi Qadarites in Basra, though they accepted the prerogatives of the Quraysh, did so only on condition that the Quraysh prove worthy of them by behaving in a fair and exemplary manner. That relation to the Basrian Qadarite movement, which, through the figure of 'Amr b. 'Ubayd, lay at the root of Mu'tazilism, explains why Dirār conceded at least implicitly that the caliph could be deposed by the community.

That was theory, as I have said. Dirār knew that for caliphs and government officials, *kuttāb,* the matter was seen in a different light, and he was prepared to accept it, for he was not a rebel. When he came to speak of his own time, his tone changed. The ruler guarantees the integration and harmony of society, he said; that is why subjects owe him obedience.[20] That ideal of well-intentioned government, of the enlightened ruler, so to speak, was apparently developed under al-Ma'mūn's reign in particular. Dirār's Mu'tazilite successors, Abū 'l-Hudhayl and al-Nazzām, seem to have offered additional nuances. Like his predecessors, al-Ma'mūn considered himself the heir to the Prophet. In addition, he liked to play the role of teacher, of pastor keeping watch over his flock (*ra'iyya*)—that is, over the community of believers. The *Risālat al-Khamīs* refers to him as the people's guide, *imām al-hudā,* inspired by divine instruction. That *risāla,* or treatise, appeared at a timely moment.

It was composed in AH 198, hence shortly after the death of al-Ma'mūn's brother al-Amīn, and in the office of al-Fadl b. Sahl, who was al-Ma'mūn's vizier in Marv, Khorāsān, where the caliph was residing at the time. The ruler did not reign by force, therefore; he influenced his subjects by virtue of his superior judgment. It was precisely his qualifications as a teacher that placed him just below the Prophet, in the position of heir, so to speak. It seems that the Mu'tazilite theologians who developed these ideas were influenced by the Iranian tradition. Education and exhortation were already central categories for Ibn al-Muqaffa'; he expressed them in his *Risāla fī 'l-sahāba*. And the *ta'dīb al-'āmma*, the duty to lead the people to their salvation—the *islāh*, as it was called—played a role in the mirrors of princes that were translated from Persian. Consider in particular the Testament of Ardashir, *'Ahd Ardashīr*, which al-Ma'mūn chose as a basic text for educating his nephew al-Wāthiq.[21]

The *mihna* soon showed how easy it was to abuse that ideal to justify violence. After the experience of the inquisition and persecution, the premise that formed the basis for pedagogical optimism was more clearly recognized: the conviction that the man in the street cannot decide for himself. The people—the masses, we would now say—are rapacious and ignorant, al-Jāhiz tells us, and that is why prophets and rulers are needed. In a similar vein, al-Qāsim b. Ibrāhīm, the Zaydī imam who was nearly a contemporary of al-Jāhiz, said that if by chance people do not express their rage against one another, it is not because they restrain themselves, but because God in his wisdom never leaves them without a teacher. Bishr b. al-Muʿtamir compares them to wolves always seeking their own advantage; this is close to the theme of *homo homini lupus* familiar to us through Thomas Hobbes. Bishr's pessimism can be explained by his personal experience. He had tried to introduce the Muʿtazilite doctrine to groups of ordinary people. He had wanted to evangelize them, particularly with popular poems, and his audience would not hear of it.[22] Thus he was disappointed. The Muʿtazilites thought they had a civilizing mission; they felt obliged to fight the *taqlīd*, conformity, of the masses and, like many others, they failed. They had projected their ideal onto the caliphs, and the caliphs too had failed to live up to it. Both groups, the caliphs and the court theologians, were soon disenchanted. "A hundred years of tyranny are better than one day of civil war": that was the only positive lesson the masses were able to draw from all those efforts at education. The maxim was mentioned by Yaʿqūbī, a

Shiite author who compromised with a Sunni regime that espoused views opposed to his.

In fact, the gap between the government and the masses widened. Instead of looking to the court, ordinary people increasingly relied on the ones who had always been generous with the advice they needed in their everyday affairs, namely, the ulema. Al-Ma'mūn, it seems, was the last Muslim ruler in the classical age to have tried to form society to fit his own ideas. After him, the government no longer felt sure of its competency. In later generations, caliphs such as al-Qādir, for example, or later, al-Nāsir, did take action, but they could do so only with the support of jurists. That did not prevent people from recognizing the authority of the government as such. In general, it was accepted as a natural fact or as an institution desired by God. Even the Shiites decided to collaborate or at least to adopt a quietist attitude. But on the far left of the doctrinaire spectrum, so to speak, there had always been the idea that the caliph was wholly unnecessary because the people could govern themselves.

At first, that was the attitude of the Khārijites in particular. But the idea did not remain confined to the periphery. In the late second century AH, it took hold at the center of the community, following the conflict between al-Amīn and al-Ma'mūn. During the unrest that broke out in Baghdad after al-Amīn's death, when al-Ma'mūn was still in Marv, the population of the capital had had to take matters into their own hands. Under the order of a certain Sahl b. Salāma, they had even formed a private army, a sort of middle-class militia paid primarily by the merchants, who were always the first victims of pillaging. Sahl b. Salāma seems to have been linked to the Muʿtazilites.[23] In fact, the theoretical model corresponding to that reality was presented by theologians of the Muʿtazilite current. In utopian terms, a leaderless community, an Islam without a caliph, could always be imagined, and utopia was gaining strength at a time when disappointment with reality was spreading. After the fall of the Umayyads, the Abbasids had claimed they were inaugurating a new era by means of a *dawla,* a turning point, a *revolution* in the original sense of the term. But in the long run the question remained whether they had really been successful. Dirār had toyed with the idea of replacing the caliph of the Quraysh tribe with a weaker candidate. Some of his colleagues developed even more radical models. The thesis at the time was that the community did not need a leader, an imam, at all, except in case of emergency—during a war for example. For the most part, it could do without one. Believers simply had to abide by the Koran. Scripture offers enough instruction to build a strict society. That position has fundamentalist overtones; it implies that the community, the believers, are capable of interpreting the Koran and that all of them would do so in the same way. But that idea was formulated by a theologian, al-Nazzām, who sought to establish ties with the court of al-Ma'mūn.[24] It seems, therefore, that he hoped that the community would confer power on the ones who knew how to interpret scripture—that is, the ulema.

In fact, he was not the first to propose that idea, and it was not only the growing ambitions of his profession that pushed him in that direction. It would be somewhat bold to maintain that he was still inspired by a tribal model in which the sheikh is the primus inter pares; for if there was anyone in Baghdad society at that time who represented the typical middle-class man and urban intellectual, it was certainly al-Nazzām. Still, the model found support among the Khārijites. The followers of Najda b. 'Āmir believed that the community did not need an imam, provided it followed the commandments of the Koran. In Iraq, it was the *Ibādiyya* in Basra that, with its senate, the *jamā'at al-muslimīn*, showed how a commercial empire could be managed by a group of notables who were both merchants and scholars. Al-Nazzām's immediate source of inspiration, however, seems to have been al-Asamm, a Mu'tazilite who lived in Basra. As we have seen, he demanded that the ruler be supported by the consensus, or *ijmā'*, of the whole community. He added that if absolutely necessary—when that unanimous agreement could not be achieved—the *umma* could do without a common leader.[25]

Al-Asamm also recognized that this model—a Presbyterian model, so to speak—suited small and local communities rather than an empire such as the Abbasid. But the conclusion he drew was true to form: he recommended decentralization. He may have done so because he had witnessed the division of the empire under Hārūn al-Rashīd. The caliph's decision had certainly been disputed. The harmful consequences of such a policy—that is, the civil war between al-Amīn and al-Ma'mūn—appeared only after al-Asamm was at the end of his career and close to death. A century earlier, the Medinese jurist Sa'īd b. al-Musayyab had also refused to swear an oath of allegiance, a *bay'a,* to two sons of 'Abd al-Malik during their father's lifetime. Al-Nazzām, for his part, lived a generation after al-Asamm; he thus experienced the unrest and anarchy that erupted in Baghdad after al-Amīn's murder. During those years, the jurists administered justice without being officially recognized by the state. In essence, people at the time were living in a society without a caliph.

That unusual situation—organized anarchy, so to speak—did not last long. The jurists apparently justified their independent decisions as the application of the "obligation to command the good." Al-Ma'mūn put an end to that development after he returned to Baghdad in AH 204. Basically, he had a great deal of respect for the scholars; he invited them to his court and liked to hold discussions with them.[26] But he did not grant them any particular role in government affairs. During the *mihna* they were forced to follow his directives. It may be that at a certain point al-Wāthiq granted them the role they wanted, that of keeping order. As the Mu'tazilite sources tell us, he may have proposed adding religious counselors to his group of officials, especially to those who were responsible for collecting taxes. Hence, he may have tried to make the *kuttāb* and the ulema cooperate with each other.[27] If that is not a legend, it was certainly a futile wish. Over time, even the Mu'tazilites distanced themselves from the government. The tide had turned, and the ascetic element associated with their thought since the beginning grew stronger.

That current reached its peak with a group that one of the sources calls the *sūfiyyat al-Mu'tazila*.[28] They rejected not only the state in the sense of a central government, but also the "world"—that is, commerce or any sort of profitable activity. The power-money combination was suspect to them. This was an urban movement. When these Mu'tazilite Sufis spoke of profit, they were thinking of merchants and tradespeople, perhaps also of artisans, but not of peasants. Satan plants his banner in the marketplace, according to a hadith. As a result, not only was the caliph's role reduced to nothing but establishing order; order as such was corrupt. The *dār al-islām* was no longer a sound, intact world; mores had changed so much that it could only be called *dār al-kufr* or *dār al-fisq*. Power was merely the result of a usurpation.

At first, the Sufis were probably merely following their *wara'*, their fear of dealing with impure and dubious things. The state, *al-sultān,* was counted among the *shubuhāt,* suspect things. The Sufis did not accept a salary from the government; they did not serve it as soldiers; they even abstained from consuming food from the princes' lands and from frequenting baths built with government money on a usurped piece of

land.[29] Those who had such scruples were not necessarily Muʿtazilites. On the contrary: Ibn Hanbal tells
similar stories in his *K. al-Waraʿ*, as does Muhāsibī in
his *K. al-Makāsib*. But it is also not possible to say that
the Muʿtazilites remained apart from these ascetic
currents. They were not the indifferent rationalists
we imagine them to be. Jaʿfar b. Harb, a Baghdad
Muʿtazilite who had served in the army, had a spiritual crisis and went to be purified in the Tigris River.
Then he dressed in new clothes he had received from
the man who had converted him to his new life,
Murdār, also a Muʿtazilite. He refused his father's inheritance because the father had been a government
employee.[30] After the *mihna* failed, and under the
reign of al-Mutawakkil, the Muʿtazilites also had to
adjust to seeing the government form pacts with
non-Muʿtazilite forces—hence, with those they considered heretics. As al-Jubbāʾī said in the late third
century, Baghdad and Egypt had become a land of
heresy, *dār kufr*, because no one could live there without professing the eternal nature of the Koran and
determinism. He himself had left the capital and Iraq
to live in Iran, in ʿAskar Mukram, where the majority
of the population still followed his doctrine.

Let me stop there. The attitude of the *sūfiyyat al-
Muʿtazila* had no future. That radical refusal led to an

impasse and in Iraq Mu'tazilism in general ceased to exert a consistent influence. The majority of Muslims agreed that government *(al-imām)*, despite its imperfection, was indispensable for the operation of society. In the long run, absolute refusal was practiced only by itinerant dervishes, *qalandar.*[31] As far as theory was concerned, the theologians soon lost the initiative to the philosophers. Thinkers such as al-Fārābī introduced completely new models. And over time the new models were confronted with new experiences: the weakening of the caliphate by the Buyids and the Seljuks, which could be explained only by a dualist model in which authority and power were carefully distinguished; the annihilation of the caliphate itself under the Mongols, the first period in the eastern world when domination was seized from Muslim hands completely; and finally the military regimes of the Mamluk period. It is easy to see that in one way or another almost all these models have parallels in the contemporary world. But that is not my subject here. The telling fact is that even today, when people have hopes, they turn to the past, as the early Mu'tazilite theologians once did. Islam began with a great political success, and it remains forever tied to that success.

5

THEOLOGY AND ITS PRINCIPLES

Hermeneutics and Epistemology

THE RELATIONSHIP—the contradiction—between faith and knowledge has always preoccupied Christianity. One believes things one cannot prove. "Credibile est quia ineptum est," said Tertullian of the incarnation: it is believable because it is absurd. And he added, "certum est quia impossible," it is certain because it is impossible. Of course, we must take into consideration the fact that the Roman Church Father was a rhetorician and not a philosopher. The famous *credo quia absurdum* does not appear in the sources before Kierkegaard, who was the first to introduce the cult of the unknowable, which was taken up by Albert Camus and existentialism.[1] But it is clear that where the incarnation was concerned, Muslims always had the impression that their Christian brothers were clinging to an illusion. Christianity speaks of the "mysteries" of faith; Islam has nothing like that. For Saint Paul, reason belongs to the realm of the "flesh"; for Muslims, reason, *'aql*, has always been the chief faculty granted human beings by God. Of course, this was not the independent reason characteristic of the Enlightenment period, but rather an intelligence subject to the will of God and to the order established by him. Still, that divine gift was accepted and appreciated everywhere, even among ascetics and mystics. Al-Hārith al-Muhāsibī, who supplies one of the first definitions of intelligence, bases his psychological analysis on it, an analysis that has earned the admiration of Sufis even in our own time.[2] Only the application of intelligence was subject to debate. Al-Muhāsibī did not like disputations *(munāzarāt);* conversely, they were the driving force of the Mu'tazilites' activities.

Let us acknowledge that some theologians doubted the validity of the methods employed by reason. Sometimes they went so far as to cultivate a sort of irrationalism. The first to be catalogued in the sources were Sufis—but also, surprisingly, Mu'tazilites. They belonged to the *sūfiyyat al-Mu'tazila* I have already mentioned, and their social criticism was directed at the theologians themselves, at their intellectual arrogance. This arrogance overlooked the fact that fundamentally no theological speculations could surpass the simple faith of the masses. How does one know what one knows? they asked, especially given that arguments for and against a particular assertion often contradict each other. All proofs have the same value—this is the famous equivalence among proofs *(takāfu' al-adilla)*, which Abū Hayyān al-Tawhīdī still refers to with some sympathy. The term, and the practice associated with it, seem to have originated in the *isostheneia tōn logōn* of Greek skepticism, whose apogee was marked by the figure of the "archheretic" Ibn al-Rāwandī.[3] But that wave of anti-intellectualism was not representative. The *sūfiyyat al-Mu'tazila* vanished without a trace, and Ibn al-Rāwandī, despite the emphatic rebuttal directed at him over several generations, did not exert any influence. Essentially, Muslims had their own methods and relied on those.

The Mu'tazilites were convinced that Wāsil b. 'Atā' had already developed a short "discourse on method." A summary of it, consisting of only a few sentences, was preserved by Qādī 'Abd al-Jabbār and, with a few variants, by his contemporary Abū Hilāl al-'Askarī in his *Kitāb al-Awā'il*.[4] We cannot rule out the possibility that the text is fiction, a projection derived from a later position, and in certain places it seems to have been reworked, but these revisions themselves lead us to think that fundamentally it is an authentic kernel of a discussion held in the early days of Muslim theology.[5] Wāsil begins with the criterion for truth. In the first place, truth is truthfulness. It is presented in the form of trustworthy propositions. Any proposition is worthy of trust when it is uttered by several people who could not have agreed on it in advance. After that, one is obliged to weigh the content of the sentence recognized as true; it may be either general or particular. That distinction was derived from the legal exegesis of the Koran, and hence of a text for which the question of trust did not arise, at least not for a Muslim. For that reason, Wāsil added a remark on abrogation *(naskh)*, a procedure that at the time concerned only scripture. His text defines it in a way that would henceforth be considered a given and which might have already been in use beforehand—namely, that only verses that are legal in nature can be abrogated, not those which speak of the world beyond or of the historical past.[6] The passage of this text that would later become the most important comes at the end: it is a brief enumeration of sources of knowledge. Among these, Wāsil lists the Koran first, inasmuch as it is precise in meaning *(muhkam)* and not ambiguous (*mutashābih;*

compare sura 3:7). Next, he lists the propositions or reports *(akhbār)* that according to the criterion mentioned above have the value of argument. And finally, he lists "sound" reason—that is, judgments not based simply on something given in advance but obtained independently through personal reflection. Wāsil says simply, *bi-ʿaql salīm.* He does not specify the procedure as being "argument" (or "reflection"), *nazar* (as later theologians would say), or *ijtihād,* independent reasoning (as the jurists would have said). In the enumeration in question, those two realms were not yet separate.

The list—assuming it is in fact that old—influenced both theologians and jurists. Among the Muʿtazilites, for example, al-Jāhiz borrowed from it and reformulated it; among the jurists, Shāfiʿī is our best witness.[7] He never cites Wāsil, of course; but when Shāfiʿī came to Baghdad to make his career, he could no longer ignore the Muʿtazilites, the *ahl al-kalām,* as he called them in his treatises. The chief disciple he acquired in the capital, Abū ʿAbd al-Rahmān al-Shāfiʿī, was a student of Abū ʾl-Hudhayl and followed Muʿtazilite doctrine. As an employee of Ibn Abī Duwād, he played an active role in the inquisition, the *mihna.*[8] We cannot overlook Shāfiʿī, because the list marks the beginning of the concept of *usūl al-fiqh* (the foundations of jurisprudence), which he is generally considered to have originated. What Wāsil and Shāfiʿī had in common was that they disregarded consensus, *ijmāʿ;* Shāfiʿī moved away from his predecessor in his definition of *khabar*.[9] For Wāsil, *khabar* designates any proposition received from another person, whereas Shāfiʿī, as a jurist, is interested in the *khabar* only as hadith and sunna.[10] Later, al-Jāhiz maintained a position between the two. He knew that hadith was indispensable for jurists, but as a Muʿtazilite he did not like it. In place of *khabar,* which in the meantime had become too ambiguous, he spoke of a "sunna accepted by all," *al-sunna al-mujmaʿ ʿalayhā*. Although he introduced the notion of *ijmāʿ,* consensus, with that expression, he did so only verbally, without granting it the status of an independent notion.

In the end, theology used other criteria. The Koran never constituted its central evidence. Muslims were living in a pluralist society, and non-Muslims could not be persuaded by quotations drawn from Koranic revelation. Theology had an apologetic task, among other roles, and that task could be performed only through reason. And the way to deal with the Koran, the way to apply the hermeneutics of commentary *(tafsīr)* to it, was well known. Several Muʿtazilite theologians wrote commentaries on the holy book, especially those belonging to the generation preceding al-Ashʿarī. Al-Jubbāʾi and Abū ʾl-Qasīm al-Balkhī did so, as did his contemporary Abū Muslim al-Isfahānī, but, even earlier, so did al-Asamm, and before him ʿAmr b. ʿUbayd, who collected Hasan al-Basrī's courses in exegesis.[11] From the beginning, the method was realistic, sober, and entirely exempt from the fanciful allegories of Origen, for example. The desire was to reconstruct the historical situation of the revelation, the *asbāb al-nuzūl,* or to take into account the precise implications of a rule extracted from the law. The practical approach can be explained, on one hand, by the desire to organize an entire complex society in accordance with the commandments of God and, on the other, by the fact that Muslims had only one book of scripture and not two like the Christians. The Church Fathers were always confronted with the problem of submitting the Old Testament to the demands of the New. Muslims, by contrast, though they respected the Bible, did not read it; it was "abrogated" and set aside for the "people of the Book," that is, for those who did not want to accept the new version brought forth by the Prophet.

There were two words for what Muslims were doing: *tafsīr* and *ta'wīl*. Both were in the Koran; scripture had reflected upon itself.[12] Koranic metalanguage was possible because the community knew the procedure from the past. *Tafsīr* was derived from the Aramaic *pishrā* and the Hebrew *pēsher*.[13] *Ta'wīl* was a different case: the word was of Arabic origin but was determined by its Koranic context. The line from sura 3:7, where the notion is developed, says that "no one knows its exegesis except God" [translation modified]: that is, no one knows how to interpret the ambiguous and complicated passages *(mutashābihāt)* previously mentioned. This could be understood as a warning: Anyone trying to interpret them will fall into heresy. As a result, the word acquired a negative connotation: *ta'wīlāt* was equated with *bida'* (innovations) or *ahwā'* (aberrations, vagaries).[14] But that was not always the case. Al-Māturīdī called his commentary of the Koran *Ta'wīlāt ahl al-sunna* (The interpretations of the people of the sunna). Later, interpretation was associated with the allegorical speculations of people such as the Ismailis, who sought a hidden meaning *(bātin)* in the Koran. The Shiites always had a certain predilection for exegetical "secrets"; they were ill used by historical reality and sought to justify their utopian ideas.

* * *

Hadith was different. The Muʿtazilites were scrip-
turalists, like the Khārijites; in their view, the tradition of the Prophet could only introduce chaos into
the sacred text. In fact, hadith, the "oral Torah" *(tōrā
shel be-pē),* so to speak, was not canonically fixed; it
was part of an oral tradition teeming with contradictions. Dirār b. ʿAmr, and al-Nazzām after him, collected striking examples of them.[15] It was Ibn
Qutayba who finally managed to resolve the contradictions in his treatise *Differences among the Hadith
(Taʾwīl mukhtalif al-hadīth).* Unlike the Koran, hadith
always suffered from a lack of reliability. The "tradition of the Prophet" *(sunnat al-nabī)* did enjoy enormous success later on, but it owed its victory to its
pure and unavoidable necessity. The theologians,
who did not need the tradition as much as the jurists, continued to require that the criteria of truth
be applied to it. As we have seen, Wāsil had asked
that those reporting a saying not come to a prior
agreement with one another. Abū ʾl-Hudhayl had introduced a numerical postulate: The number of witnesses guaranteed certainty. Quantity was thus transformed into quality. But he immediately recognized
the inadequacy of that rule. The number had to be
specified, and no one could do that without being
challenged. The solution could only be an act of will.

Abū 'l-Hudhayl decided on twenty people. As evidence, he simply modified a Koranic verse that spoke of jihad rather than of knowledge: "If there are twenty steadfast men among you, they shall vanquish two hundred."[16] That analogy was extremely weak, being founded on an arbitrarily chosen resemblance, a *qiyās al-shabah,* as the jurists would have said. Above all, a hadith cannot be transmitted by just any multitude; it is a sacred text and belongs to the tradition of the *umma.* The twenty people must therefore be Muslims, "friends of God," or, as Abū 'l-Hudhayl seems to have said, "candidates for paradise" *(min ahl al-janna).* We do not know whether he thought he would find these "candidates" among his contemporaries or in the generation of the Companions of the Prophet; the sources are too vague to allow us to determine that. But the profound skepticism in his words is obvious. He spoke of certainty, and for him the only things that were certain were truths such as the existence of God, prophecy, and the experience of the senses. Words alone would never be capable of achieving certainty; they could only be probable. Regarding that probability, Abū 'l-Hudhayl was much more generous: four people were sufficient. That placed the question within the domain of jurists. He may have been thinking of the four witnesses required in cases of adultery.[17]

The advocates of hadith could not be satisfied with that arrangement. Many legal rules were based on a hadith attested by a single chain of transmitters, a *khabar al-wāhid*. In the long run, those unique hadith, *āhād* as they were called, became a problem. The jurist 'Īsā b. Abān (d. AH 221/836 CE), a disciple of Shaybānī and an influential man in the court of Hārūn al-Rashīd, seems to have written the first monograph on the question.[18] Shāfi'ī considered them indispensable; he devoted a long chapter of his *Risāla* to them.[19] But even by the looser criteria of a jurist, they were difficult to justify; to be valid, testimony normally had to be supplied by at least two people. An additional criterion had to be agreed on, therefore: the transmitter's integrity, or *'adāla*. The Mu'tazilites accepted that criterion from the beginning; Wāsil had spoken of it. For them, however, it was primarily a category of public life, regulating the "cohabitation" of people in politics, for example. To consider someone a person of integrity meant that you trusted him. Nevertheless, despite the existence of trust, verification was better. So it was that in place of the witness's reliability, al-Nazzām proposed verification by context, concomitant facts (qarā'in) that lent support to the veracity of a report. In doing so, he was still thinking within the framework established by Wāsil, for his examples had to do with news of the day: for example, one heard of a neighbor's death and also saw a coffin set out in front of his house.[20] Like many others, al-Nazzām did not yet take the trouble to point out what was unique about hadith. There, context was less important because the reports regularly resurfaced over time along the chain of transmission, the isnād. It was his disciple Jāhiz who first focused on hadith. In pursuing his master's thinking, he added that the collective experience of a community accumulates in the tradition. Unfortunately, that experience deteriorates as a result of transmission, and in the end God finds himself obliged to send a new messenger.[21]

Al-Nazzām was the archetype of the rationalist, as his reactions constantly show. He did not believe in the existence of jinni, and he rejected the popular interpretation of dreams and omens.[22] But he was also the first to prove the prophethood of Muhammad by predictions found in the Koran. He believed that the Prophet was gifted with a miraculous knowledge of the occult and of the future (ghayb). Indeed, the events the Prophet had foretold were borne out in accounts. Some of these were historical, such as the short-lived triumph of the Byzantines over the Sassanids alluded to in sura 30:1–3, whereas others were literary, such as the stoning of devils by shooting stars or comets (sura 67:5, 15:16–17, among other verses), for which proof was sought in pre-Islamic poetry.[23] In opening the door to miracles halfway, he set off an avalanche. The next generation of Mu'tazilites would concern themselves with countless narratives on the subject, and not only those about Muhammad's exploits mentioned in the sacred text itself. There were also many in Ibn Ishāq's *Sīra* and in other texts. 'Abbād b. Sulaymān felt he could no longer ignore all that material. Miracles had become the principal tool for demonstrating Muhammad's truthfulness, just as they had always been for Jesus among the Christians. 'Abbād claimed that these events that surpassed the grasp of reason were true because they were sometimes recounted by people as irreproachable *(ma'sūm)* as the Prophet himself. That argument allowed him more confidently to adopt the postulate of the people of paradise, *ahl al-janna,* formulated by Abū 'l-Hudhayl.[24] The people to whom he was alluding were probably the Companions. As already mentioned, his master, Hishām al-Fuwatī (who had himself been a disciple of Abū 'l-Hudhayl), took an important step toward canonizing the Companions, the *sahāba*. He did so in political theory but anticipated the consequences of that move for historiography.

In essence, *ijmā'* bore only a marginal relation to epistemology. In its epistemological manifestation, Aristotle included it within the "famous" or well-known opinions accepted by everyone, the *mashhūrāt* in Ibn Sinā's later terminology.[25] In Islam, the concept originally belonged rather to the political arena. *Ijmā'* was closer to consultation, *shūrā*. When, according to a text in Wakī''s *Akhbār al-qudāt*, 'Umar b. 'Abd al-'Azīz recommended that his Basrian governor 'Adī b. Artāt consult competent, discerning people in cases where the Koran, the sunna, and the practice of caliphs no longer provided any solution, 'Umar was speaking in principle only of a consensus, *ijmā'*, of local scholars.[26] As early as the pre-Islamic era, a tribal chief could not make a decision simply on his own whim; he was obliged to follow procedure by eliciting a consensus. Al-Asamm, who was the first of the Mu'tazilites to grant a key position to *ijmā'*, recommended it primarily as a political instrument to establish the validity of the oath of allegiance, or *bay'a*.[27]

But just as they are in our own societies, political decisions were open to judicial review, at least after the fact. Practice had to submit to the test of theoretical validity. It was thus integrated into a new context—that, indeed, of epistemology. In jurisprudence, *ijmā'* more or less corresponded to the sunna understood in the sense of "local custom"; we need only compare the consensus of Medinese scholars in Mālik b. Anas's writings to be assured of that. It is known in the same form in Shāfi'ī's writings, as we have seen; Shāfi'ī considers *ijmā'* an additional confirmation and not an independent criterion. For him, the word generally means only agreement among specialists on the interpretation of a text, and this text is often a sunna.[28] Argument, therefore, always depends on the sunna. Compared to the omnipresent authority of one of the Prophet's sayings, the authority of an *ijmā'* was rather limited. The opinion of Shāfi'ī was shared outside Medina by many other ancient jurists—Awzā'ī, for example, or Abū Yūsuf.[29] For the Mu'tazilites who did not value hadith, the situation appeared in a different light. For them, *ijmā'* could replace the sunna rather than simply confirm it. Dirār b. 'Amr, for example, considers it the only criterion besides the Koran. In a sense, Dirār even granted it a higher place than the Koran itself, for it was not clear, given the ambiguity of scripture and the problem of abrogation and *mutashābihāt*, on which passage of scripture a judgment ought, without the unanimous support of the community, to be based. People would simply set one *auctoritas* against another, as they did in hadith.[30] Later, when the Mu'tazilites had lost their battle against the Prophetic tradition and had to accept it as a source, they called *ijmā'* "the proposition of the community," *khabar al-umma*, as opposed to the proposition of the Prophet, *khabar al-nabī*—that is, hadith.[31]

We therefore arrive at a rather paradoxical result: *ijmā'*, which later became the Sunni principle par excellence, was first propagated absolutely and without restrictions by those who would be considered heretics in later centuries—that is, by the Mu'tazilites. The situation was complicated by the fact that the parties opposing *ijmā'* were also recruited from groups that were unorthodox in their time, the Khārijites and the Shiites. But these cases were different; unlike the Mu'tazilites, they had always been excluded from the political coalition. In addition, the Khārijites had severed themselves from the community before it had even acquired a coherent shape. As a result, they were more literalist than the Mu'tazilites. They did not punish adultery with stoning, they did not practice *mash 'alā 'l-khuffayn,* the practice of rubbing the shoes instead of the feet during ritual cleansing, and they inexorably cut off thieves' hands without recognizing the exceptions through which jurists attenuated the rigor of the Koran. That, at least, is what 'Abd al-Qāhir al-Baghdādī said.[32] The reality may have been more complex than it appeared. They wanted to have nothing in common with those they had abandoned. But they, of course, established solidarity among themselves; there is reason to believe that "the community of believers" of Basrian Ibadites, the *jamā'at al-muslimīn,* proceeded by consensus of a sort, though it was still on a political level. As for the Shiites, they were disappointed because they had been in the minority since the time of the Companions. During the caliphate of Abū Bakr and 'Umar, the consensus of the community had not favored 'Alī. In jurisprudence, the Shiites always indicated their preference for *ijtihād,* independent reasoning. There, the vote of the majority lost much of its value very early on.

Among the Mu'tazilites, criticism emerged only with al-Nazzām. He was accused of having been influenced by the Shiites, but in reality he was reacting against the "people of hadith," *ashāb al-hadīth,* who had begun to base the *ijmā'* on a hadith: "My com-

munity will never reach agreement on an error."[33]
That saying was demonstrably apocryphal. Shāfiʿī
does not cite it.[34] Its content reminds us of the role
played by the Holy Spirit in Christianity. "The
Church of Rome does not make mistakes," Pope
Lucius I is supposed to have said, according to the
Pseudo-Isidorian Decretals. By disseminating the
hadith cited, Muslims reassured themselves that they
were orthodox. Dissension, *ikhtilāf*, had always been
considered characteristic of sects and infidels. In addition, the infidels not only disagreed among themselves, they also filled their imaginations with collective errors. Christians, for example, all agreed with
the assertion that Jesus had died on the cross—which
was clearly false, according to the Koran. The Jews
were convinced that the revelation transmitted to
Moses had never been abrogated, a belief that was refuted by the existence of Islam. But is it true that
such errors had never occurred among Muslims?
Jāhiz, following in al-Nazzām's footsteps, noted that
during the caliphate of al-Mansūr, in Bahrain (which
at the time covered the entire eastern coast of the
Persian Gulf), the whole population prayed as a community on Thursdays—hence, the day before the prescribed day. Al-Nazzām adopted a sarcastic tone in
expressing his view on the subject: if a group of blind

people are brought together, they see no better than they did before. All Muslims believe, for example, that Muhammad was the only prophet sent to the whole world. Yet reason shows us that that is false; for all prophets—Jesus, Moses, and the others— proved their authenticity through miracles, and a miracle is perceived by the senses and is thus addressed to human beings as such. The *ijmā'* is, then, nothing but an illusion. But that sort of ruthless skepticism not only destroyed *ijmā'*, it had consequences for hadith. By analogy, a report cannot become reliable by the mere fact of having had several chains of transmission *(mutawātir)*.[35]

Al-Nazzām was intelligent but was found to be a bit too capricious. Jāhiz, the first of the Mu'tazilites to distance himself from his master's doctrines, describes his character.[36] Khayyāt, who lived a generation later, claims that in Baghdad no one shared al-Nazzām's views any longer. Yet another generation later, Abū Hāshim accepted the hadith mentioned above, which al-Nazzām had ridiculed. He was determined to accept the *ijmā'*, and no "authority" supported it, except this hadith and a few passages from the Koran, which were however much too vague.[37] As the time of open options receded into the past, people increasingly felt the need for an agreement on true custom. Al-Nazzām had still made fun of the Companions of the Prophet and of their internecine quarrels, but immediately after his death political correctness took hold in regard to the sacred past, even in the Muʿtazilite school.[38] To al-Nazzām, the disputes among the Companions still seemed normal; discord was life, and human beings had received intellect to help them find their own bearings. After him, that attitude became untenable. The Muʿtazilites never stopped praising reason, but now limits were placed on the breaking of taboos. Qāḍī ʿAbd al-Jabbār would later say that even though the *umma*'s infallibility cannot be proved, one must not conclude that it will necessarily commit errors.

The "sound reason" Wāsil had spoken of was not yet al-Nazzām's arrogant rationalism. What Wāsil had in mind was the good sense of the jurists. People remembered that among these jurists were virtuosi who had in their time dazzled the masses with their wisdom and subtlety: Iyās b. Muʿāwiya, for example, or, before him, Shaʿbī.[39] These men had a gift for judging a situation intuitively, by *firāsa*, with perspicacity. But they did not yet have a method, and even less a discourse on it. They employed analogies but relied in doing so on their knowledge of human beings, without invoking any explicit rule. At the time, jurisprudence was at the forefront, having come into its own partly thanks to the instrument of the fatwa. No one was writing manuals yet, but people were trying to analyze specific situations that had not been clarified. Each community, each "sect," had its own specialist. In Mecca, there were specialists on pilgrims. Texts are available to help us reconstitute that forgotten culture: the *al-Jawābāt* (Responses) by Jābir b. Zayd al-Azdī (d. AH 93/712 CE), or the *al-Aqwāl Qatāda*, summaries of juridical decisions made by Qatāda b. Diʿāma (d. AH 117?/735 CE?).[40] Unfortunately, they were neglected because they were "sectarian," alien to the dominant trend in later centuries. The "method" revealed in them is *ra'y* (literally, "opinion"), a mode of thought that followed the logic of the situation without constantly appealing to an independent authority, but which was opposed to pure whim and arbitrary decisions *(hawā)*.

The verb used in combination with *ra'y* was *ijtahada*, "to exert oneself"; *ijtahada ra'yahū* meant "to form an opinion about something."[41] In the long run, the term *ra'y* lost its positive connotations. It was associated with the al-Kufa school, the followers of Abū Hanīfa who had stayed closest to the principles of ancient tradition in Iraq. In Basra, a town with a complex intellectual outlook, the term *ijtihād* replaced *ra'y,* and people began to concern themselves with the specific reason, *'illa,* that justified the procedure applied.[42] Those who did so came from different "disciplines." 'Uthmān al-Battī was a contemporary of Abū Hanīfa and corresponded with him. Abū Hanīfa sent him his famous Epistle, *Risāla.*[43] 'Uthmān's response was that of a jurist, 'Amr b. 'Ubayd's that of a theologian, and the response of 'Abdallāh b. Abī Ishāq al-Hadramī, who was a generation older than the two others (d. AH 117/735 CE), that of a grammarian.[44] In the beginning, however, the Basrian *ijtihād* was taken to extremes, just as the *ra'y* was in al-Kufa. 'Ubaydallāh b. al-Hasan al-'Anbarī (d. AH 168/785 CE), a disciple of Iyās b. Mu'āwiya, formulated the following maxim: "Whoever forms an opinion (and is capable of doing so) is right," *kull mujtahid musīb.*[45] Muslims had suddenly arrived at pluralism—and, it appeared, at relativism.

The expert's independence was never so confidently asserted as at that time. 'Anbarī did not distinguish between jurisprudence and theology. He chose his examples from both fields at once. *Mash 'alā 'l-khuffayn,* shoe-rubbing, could be either accepted or rejected, he said; but he also maintained that someone who defends free will is just as right as someone who believes in predestination. He always chose problems that had not been definitively solved by the Koran, the only authority 'Anbarī seems to have accepted. For theology, that position turned out to be untenable. Eternal truths could not be subject to the caprices of the human intellect (though they were in reality). In the *fiqh,* the human attempt to understand divine law, it was a different situation. It was soon recognized that the judgment of a mufti or *qāḍī* never led to more than a certain probability *(ghalabat al-zann).* Manuals devoted to the hermeneutic foundations of the *fiqh (usūl al-fiqh)* never fail to address the subject.[46] There too, Muslims wanted to avoid indecisiveness. 'Anbarī had touched on a sensitive and important point, as the absence of appeals courts in the classical judicial system demonstrates.[47]

Yet jurists were not ready to resign themselves to uncertainty. Shāfi'ī did not yet see the situation as relating to verisimilitude. According to him, the believer, in following the law, is doing something that is either objectively correct or subjectively permitted.[48] It was the Mu'tazilites' rationalism that slowed down the process. Both al-Asamm and Bishr al-Marīsī, a very influential jurist in the court of al-Ma'mūn and the instigator of the *mihna,* as well as al-Nazzām at a later time, continued to hope that basing all legal argument on reason would be possible.[49] As for reasoning by analogy *(qiyās),* with which a casuistic system cannot dispense, al-Asamm and Bishr al-Marīsī thought they could manage the situation through a method more solid than the *'illa.*[50] At that point, however, al-Nazzām, with his usual skepticism, suggested that they were not on the right path. Not even God applied analogy—the Koran was the proof of that. According to sura 24:31, no one is allowed to see the hair of a free woman. Analogy would dictate that that is also the case for a slave woman, especially if she is beautiful (or more beautiful than the free woman). But the opposite is true, as verse 33:59 shows.[51] The Sharia is rife with such contradictions. For example, the traveler, *ibn al-sabīl,* who is exempt from prayer and fasting, must make up for only the second of these obligations, not the first.[52] Chaos is intentional, and analogy would only increase it. The Koran is beyond criticism and can only be accepted. Apart from it, the only authority is reason. It does not tell us to proceed by analogy but to take scriptural commandments literally. If a husband repudiates his wife, he must do so with the exact words mentioned in the Koran or with a sentence containing the word *talāq* (divorce); intention alone will not

suffice. In taking that position, al-Nazzām abandoned the majority opinion and arrived at a literalist,
or *zāhirite,* view.[53] Unlike his two predecessors, he was
not a practicing jurist.

Analogy, or *qiyās,* was considered a normal expression
of *ijtihād,* and was included among the four basic
principles of jurisprudence, the *usūl al-fiqh.* It was not
a "source" but a method; it belonged to the realm of
form and not of matter. In jurisprudence, its function was to support casuistic probabilism. In theology, that was not sufficient. Theologians used the
same term, but what they meant by it was *qiyās al-
ghā'ib 'alā 'l-shāhid.* Rather than an analogy, it was a
conclusion *(qīyas)* based on what was before one's
eyes, *shāhid* (that is, what was present and well
known), as compared to the hidden, *ghā'ib*—that is,
God and the hereafter. They did not admit that there
could be an analogy between God and the world. Islam has never developed the doctrine of *analogia entis,*
and the Mu'tazilites, despite all their theories about
the attributes of God, always had the utmost respect
for the affirmation of his transcendence, *tanzīh*
(aphairesis for the Greeks).[54] For the Mu'tazilites,
analogy was a manifestation not of *ijtihād* but of

istidlāl, a term they associated with the word for "proof," *dalīl. Dalīl* was nothing other than a "sign," an indication, and *qiyās* was any ratiocination whatsoever, preferably a deduction. It is for that reason that Aristotle's translators, usually Christians, took the liberty of applying the term *qiyās* to the syllogism, which in the *Organon* indicated the method for drawing conclusions *kat' exokhen.* The fact that *qiyās* was only a formal element in the jurists' tool kit facilitated the transition to philosophy, where the problems addressed were similar to those of theology. With regard to the other three "sources" of law, such an affinity did not exist.[55]

Theological knowledge was however not only a certainty; it was also—and for the same reason—a duty. The Koran emphasized that God provided the "signs" *(āyāt)* so that humankind could recognize God's existence. In a sense, a knowledge of signs was even "necessary," for they were perceived with the eyes, and sense perception was inevitable—*darūrī,* given a priori. What was "acquired" *(iktisābī)* in that process was only the conclusion, the result of moving from the *semēion (dalīl)* to the *semēioton (madlūl),* from sign to signified; but that conclusion could be drawn by anyone. One had only to desire it. What was acquired could also rightly be called *ikhtiyārī,* dependent on the choice *(ikhtiyār)* of the individual. As a result, knowledge of God became an obligation by virtue of divine law, an element of *taklīf*. It was a human act like any other. People could disagree on the way to define that act. On the subject of free will *(ikhtiyār)*, for example, Dirār b. ʿAmr had argued for a synergism that divided the elements of the human act between God and man. He thought that human beings are agents by virtue of the fact that they perform the action and "acquire" it for their own benefit *(kasb* or *iktisāb)*, whereas God creates it in that he makes it occur.[56] The Muʿtazilites did not adopt that model, but Abū ʾl-Hudhayl was one of the first to refute it.[57] He spoke of *ʿilm iktisābī*, knowledge "acquired" by theological speculation *(nazar)*.[58] And the *kasb*, "acquisition," remained forever a "cipher," a metaphor for "responsibility."[59]

The appeal to the *taklīf* produced new difficulties. If the "acquisition" of religious knowledge was obligatory, one ought not to postpone it. Every instant spent without knowledge of God and Islam was wasted. Moreover, knowledge required time; as a result, Muslims wondered what respite *(muhla)* people could have once they had reached adulthood. In that regard there was no fundamental difference between believers and pagans. Of course, Muslims took advantage of the fact that their "respite" was normally taken up by religious education, but the obligation itself was also valid for non-Muslims, and insofar as they fulfilled it, they were following God's commandment, just as believers were. Naturally, it was possible that they might remain unbelievers in spite of everything; in that case, their knowledge of truth would be only partial, and they would have fulfilled their duty without the intention that ought to accompany it. Abū 'l-Hudhayl was the first to discuss the problem. There are works of obedience, he said, by which one does not "will" God. That can also happen to Muslims. They find themselves in this predicament in the first instant of their knowledge of God, for they do not yet know that what they are doing is a meritorious act.[60]

That theorem was rather far removed from reality. Normally, education introduced the concept of merit from the beginning, alongside the first religious ideas. But the aporia hidden within it fascinated Muslims. It may therefore be possible, they said, to fulfill, without realizing it, an obligation established by God. That eventuality seems to be universal: there is no reason to limit it to the infidels, for to know that one is obliged to know God, one must already

know him. One might conclude that the notion of
God is an a priori concept. That was for a long time
the conclusion; the word for "a priori" was *fitra*.[61]
Abū 'l-Hudhayl believed it, despite the fact that he
had gone to a great deal of trouble to develop proofs
of the existence of God.[62] In his view, these proofs
were designed only to provide reassurance a posteri-
ori. But in that case one would have to concede that
pagans too possessed that prior knowledge of God,
and should one truly concede that pleasure to them?
Certain theologians argued the reverse. The consequence seemed to be that unbelievers, at least those
who had never had the opportunity to hear of God or
of Islam, were innocent. They also did not deserve
paradise, of course, but henceforth they could not be
condemned to hell. The Koran offered a third alternative: They would return to dust after their deaths.
According to sura 78:40, the polytheists of Mecca
wanted to be treated that way after their resurrection,
but to no avail. By comparison with hell, it was a
more agreeable fate. But for those who had known
the truth and rejected it, such a fate was out of the
question.

Thumāma b. Ashras, councilor and "minister
without portfolio" to the court of al-Ma'mūn, made

the same argument, and al-Jāhiz came to embrace his viewpoint.[63] But al-Jāhiz took the idea further by asserting, in a psychological approach that was revolutionary for the time, that despite the "presumption of innocence," it may still be true that everyone, Muslim or not, arrives at the knowledge of God without being initiated in advance. One must simply concede that such knowledge cannot be controlled and that it shares that distinctive character with all other types of knowledge. Above all, it need not be "produced" (*muwallad, mutawallid*) by something; it can result naturally from an act of reflection, but that is not a condition sine qua non. Our brains work in a different way; our speculations are not calculable. Hence, there is no obligation to know God.

These ideas were ingenious and infused with a subtle tolerance, but they also indicated the bankruptcy of Muʿtazilite rationalism. In reacting against that apparent flaw, al-Jubbāʾī, with his usual scholasticism, tried to prove why human beings, despite the arguments advanced by al-Jāhiz, must necessarily feel the obligation to know God. No one, he said, lacks the experience of depending on a power that governs him and to which he is beholden. To show gratitude toward this power, however, a person must know whom to address. Knowledge of God is thus as it

were the personalization of the experience of the "numinous," of an indefinite divine power.[64] That theory
too was only a hypothesis at first. A Muslim did not
need that confrontation with the numinous, nor did
the "people of the Book," the *ahl al-kitāb*, nor the majority of pagans, for they were all conditioned by the
religious ideas of their society. To support the theory,
therefore, an example had to be found or constructed. It was soon discovered in the figure of an individual living alone on an island, the Robinson Crusoe motif. Al-Jubbā'ī himself seems to have used it.
Later on, it was primarily Shiite authors who
adopted it: Kulīnī (d. AH 328/939 CE) and Ibn Bābawayh (d. AH 381/991 CE). The idea was later developed
by Ibn Tufayl. Finally, Ibn al-Nafīs granted it promi-
nence and pushed it to the point of caricature in his
Risāla al-Kāmiliyya.[65] In his narrative, the hero discov-
ers not only theological and metaphysical truths by
virtue of his intellect, but also, through the rational
necessity of prophethood, the course of human history. The location of the "Robinson Crusoe" (who is
called Kāmil, "Perfect," in Ibn al-Nafīs and Hayy b.
Yaqzān, "Living son of Awakened," in Ibn Tufayl), was
naturally a marginal detail. The Orient had various
remote places to offer: the desert (Ibn Bābawayh), a
mountaintop (Kulīnī). Only Juwaynī, an Ash'arite,

and Muhammad b. Ibrāhīm al-Kindī, an Ibadite, spoke of an island.[66]

Rationalists trusting too much in certain models may become presumptuous, if not blind and fanatical. Over time, the Muʿtazilites stopped being the friends of the masses; they hated the incapacity of the latter to understand true doctrine. Even Bishr b. al-Muʿtamir, who had tried to win over the common people with his didactic poetry, criticized their *taqlīd*, the intellectual indolence they showed—especially in not following his views.[67] His disciple al-Murdār developed the same attitude, at least for a while, until he converted to a more accessible didactic style and began to compose books intelligible to common mortals.[68] His ascetic simplicity linked him to the *sūfiyyat al-Muʿtazila*, the only ones to take a stand against intellectual arrogance. Outside the Muʿtazilite circles, Ibn Kullāb and his friends, who had endured the brutality of the *mihna*, also opted for more moderation. For them, someone incapable of articulating on his own why he is a believer can nevertheless be considered one. But even they expressed reservations. They admitted that such a person obeyed God with his faith, but they remained convinced that in spite of everything he was committing a sin because he neglected theological reflection. The *muqallid*, the one who, through his *sacrificium intellectus*, fails to find the right path, must therefore be likened to the "prevaricator," *fāsiq*.[69] Except that according to them the *fāsiq* was not in an intermediate position *(manzila bayna 'l-manzilatayn)*, as he was for the Mu'tazilites, but could place his hope in God, who in his mercy might spare the *fāsiq* the sufferings of hell.[70]

Intellectualism turned inward led to a certain quarrelsomeness. It was instigated most forcefully by public disputation, *munāzara*, where arrogance joined forces with competitiveness. The warping of the profession that resulted was typical of the *mutakallimūn*. Let us compare other kinds of religious activity. Hadith was simply transmitted. Mysticism was limited at the time to intimate contact between master and disciple. Greek philosophy and science were taught at home. Conversely, theology, because of its apologetic nature, favored public debate from the start, and that attracted curiosity-seekers and produced emotional reactions. Winning and losing were always at stake. As in the marketplace, skill and speed of reaction often prevailed over circumspection and sincerity. Al-Jāhiz saw clearly that that propensity could devolve into charlatanry. He himself, though a good writer, was far from a good public jouster. His physiognomy did not lend itself to that, and the rules of public display may have been the same as they are in modern democracies. Al-Jāhiz also recognized that in the heat of argument the line between antagonistic positions could vanish. That was not serious so long as the positions were fictive, as they were in belles lettres, *adab* (in his *Book of Animals,* he himself had invented a *disputatio* between a cock and a dog).[71] But theology was entirely different. One does not play around with the truth, and it is not enough to be right, especially by virtue of one's rhetorical skill. In the long run, the image of the *mutakallimūn* increasingly came to resemble that of a star lawyer in an American trial today. The Muʿtazilites were aware of the disadvantages. They found themselves facing a wave of resentment and antipathy. Even now, the inclination is to take the word *kalām,* from which *ʿilm al-kalām* and *mutakallimūn* are derived, to mean "pointless talk," "prattle." The simple folk had that reaction, but so did the scholars close to them, the *ashāb al-hadīth,* many jurists, and finally the philosophers themselves. Philosophers, however, reacted that way for a different reason: they thought that the style of the *kalām* corresponded to Aristotle's dialectic, a genre the Greek master had

ranked second, clearly below the apodictic art represented by syllogistic logic.[72]

How do we know what we know? Why are we right
when we are right? Men of later generations, al-
Ghazālī, for example, but also Fakhr al-Dīn al-Rāzī,
were fascinated by syllogism and had great hopes for
it. But its promise proved illusory. Ultimately, syllogism yields only what has been put into it. The conclusion depends on the premises, but who will verify
the premises? If the premises had been taken from
the Koran, the question would have been
superfluous. That was not generally the case; theologians always proceeded differently, as we have seen.
Knowledge comes from a conviction (*i'tiqād*) supported by proofs, they said. Abū 'l-Hudhayl had already made that assertion, adding that such a pre-
condition is not valid for every sort of knowledge.
Some forms of knowledge are not "produced" because they are "necessary."[73] But when they are produced, that is, when truth emerges at the end of our
reflection process, we sense it. Truth does not manifest itself through reality testing, which in any case is
not always possible in theology. Rather, it imposes itself through a subjective criterion: peace of mind
(*sukūn al-qalb*). To think, to reflect, is a movement of

the soul, said al-Nazzām, and that movement sub-
sides when one arrives at knowledge.[74] Nevertheless,
it is illusory to believe that the piece of knowledge is
true for that reason; perhaps we are simply the victims of a natural reflex. Indeed, those who err also believe they are right. Al-Jāhiz exhorted people not to
forget that; he remembered the Greek skeptics' objections.[75] It was reported that one of these skeptics, a
"sophist," had badgered Thumāma b. Ashras, in in-
sisting that every thought is only conjecture *(hisbān)*.

As a result, al-Jāhiz added an objective criterion to
al-Nazzām's approach. There are sentences, he said,
that are recognized as true not only subjectively but
also objectively, by virtue of their correspondence to
reality, their *adaequatio intellectus et rei,* as the Christian Scholastics would have said. He had discovered
the need for that adjustment when considering false
propositions. Although it is acceptable to say that
something is true because one believes it, one cannot
say that the same thing is false because one does not
believe it. There thus exist not only statements that
are true and others that are false, but also statements
that are neither true nor false, either because they do
not correspond to reality, despite the fact that someone believes them, or, conversely, because someone
says of a thing that it is objectively true, without be-

ing convinced of it. The first case is that of "innocent" pagans, the second that of "hypocrites,"
munāfiqūn.[76] Al-Jāhiz knew that his master al-Nazzām
had already referred to a Koranic verse in which a
similar case was described by God himself: "When
the hypocrites come to you [the Prophet] they say:
'We bear witness that you are God's apostle.' God
knows that you are indeed his apostle; and God bears
witness that the hypocrites are surely lying."[77] At a
certain point, then, the *munāfiqūn* had said, but without believing it, something that was true; for that
reason, they were liars. Truth and sincerity were not
the same thing, nor were lies and error. Unfortunately, at the time, the Arabic expression *kadhabta*
could mean both "you are lying" and "what you're
saying is false." Like the word *pseudos* in Greek, the
Arabic word does not distinguish between the subjective and the objective meaning.[78] But even though
there is no difference in the language, there certainly
is one in reality. Once again, al-Jāhiz took the Koran
to witness. Sura 34:8 tells us that the polytheists of
Mecca could not decide whether to consider the
Prophet a liar or a man possessed by jinni. Yet in this
context, "possessed" could only allude to someone
who says false things without knowing it.

The first to refute the "sophists," or rather, the arguments of the Greek skeptics, was another student of al-Nazzām, Muhammad b. Shabīb al-Basrī. He knew that to achieve that goal, he would have to explain sensory illusions.[79] We are familiar with the skeptics' arguments through Sextus Empiricus's treatises and through other texts. In the Muslim world, these books were still unknown, and their "sophisms" were instead spread via a "diffuse tradition" that disseminated many Greek ideas never officially translated. Those responsible for it may have been physicians: the "empirical" school that refused to base diagnoses on syllogisms had links with skepticism. But fundamentally, theologians were not dealing with sensory illusions; the problem was revelation. No one would ever succeed in explaining it and replacing it with reason. If all the elements of faith could be discovered through human reflection, why would God have spoken? That is what Ibn al-Rāwandī said, and he was not altogether wrong. If he had heard the reply to his argument that his antagonists later gave—namely, that God did so to spare his creatures a little trouble—he would have only smiled sarcastically.[80] It is true that Muslims have avoided absurdity for all time;[81] even for them, however, harmony between faith and reason remained an inaccessible ideal.

NOTES

INDEX

NOTES

Introduction

1. Or "a rationality" *('aql)*. Tāhā Husayn, *Mustaqbal al-thaqāfa fī Misr*, 2 vols. (Cairo, 1939), 1:23, fourth and fifth lines from the bottom.

2. Ibid., 63, lines 2–3.

3. Mustafā 'Abd al-Rāziq, "L'Islam et l'Occident," *Cahiers du Sud* 34 (1947): 19.

4. A. von Kügelgen, *Averroes und die arabische Moderne: Ansätze zu einer Neubegründung des Rationalismus im Islam* (Leiden, 1994).

5. Such "conversations," *takallama* and *kallama* (connected with the accusative form), were probably modeled on the Greek *dialégesthai (peri tinos)*, see my *Theologie und Gesellschaft im 2. und 3. Jahrhundert Hidschra*, 6 vols. (Berlin, 1991–1997), 1:48–49. Hereafter cited as *TG*.

6. *TG*, 3:66, 307.

7. Ibid., 299–300.

8. Ibn al-Faqīh, *Akhbār al-buldān* (Frankfurt, 1987), in *Majmū' fī 'l-jughrāfiya*, publications of the Institut

für Geschichte der Arabisch-Islamischen
Wissenschaften, C 43, p. 105, lines 4–5.

1. Theology in Its Own Eyes

1. See *TG,* 3:470–471, 4:676.
2. *TG,* 4:675; for the sister, see also 722–723.
3. Passages from the Koran are taken from the Penguin translation by N. J. Dawood (New York, 1995).—Trans.
4. According to T. Nagel, *Der Koran* (Munich, 1983), 138.
5. *TG,* 4:353–360.
6. Ibid., 680–683.
7. Ibid., 657–660.
8. Ibid., 3:390–392.
9. Ibid., 2:155–164.
10. Ibid., 4:656–657.
11. Ibid., 3:176, 4:691.
12. Ibid., 1:136–137.
13. Ibid., 1:416–443, 3:331–342.
14. Ibid., 3:20–22.
15. Ibid., 1:443–450.
16. Ibid., 417–418.
17. Ibid., 4:976, index, s.v. "Radd ʿalā ʾl-zanādiqa."
18. Ibid., 3:65.
19. Ibid., 4:269, 299–304.
20. Ibid., 3:446–481.
21. Ibid., 4:461–465.

22. Ibid., 676–678, 680–681.

23. For the origin of the term among the Shiites, see
    TG, 1:377 and 385; compare suras 4:171 and 5:77.

24. *TG*, 4:678–679, 687.

25. Abu Hāmid al-Ghazālī, *Faisal al-tafriqa bayna 'l islām
    wa'l zandaqa,* written before the *Mustasfā* and the
    Munqidh min al-dalāl, but after the *Tahāfut.*

26. *TG*, 4:677–678; for the Mamluk dynasty, see E.
    Geoffroy, *Le soufisme en Égypte et en Syrie* (Damascus,
    1995), 380–385.

27. J. C. M. Laurent, *Peregrinatores medii aevi quattuor*
    (Leipzig, 1864), 135, chap. 30, nos. 4–12.

2. Theology and the Koran

I have discussed the subject of this chapter in more detail
in *Le voyage initiatique en terre d'islam,* ed. M. A. Amir-
Moezzi (Louvain, 1996), 27–56; compare *TG*, 4:373–424,
esp. 387–391. For the problem of anthropomorphism in
general, see D. Gimaret, *Dieu à l'image de l'homme: Les
anthropomorphismes de la* sunna *et leur interprétation par les
théologiens* (Paris, 1997). Gimaret cites evidence from
hadith.

1. See especially *Le livre de l'échelle de Mahomet* (Paris,
   1991); Jamel-Eddine Bencheikh, *Le voyage nocturne de
   Mahomet* (Paris, 1988).

2. Translation has been significantly modified to con-
   form to the French. The author is following, with
   his own modifications, Jacques Berque's French

translation, *Le Coran, un nouvel essai de traduction* (Paris, 1995).—Trans.

3. A later example was al-Ghazālī in his *Mishkāt al-anwār*.

4. *TG*, 2:642, 3:450–452, 4:215.

5. Al-Tabarī, *Jāmiʿ al-bayān ʿan taʾwīl āy al-Qurʾān* (Cairo, AH 1373/1954 CE), 27:44–45.

6. Ibn ʿAbbās may have already used that argument (al-Tabarī, *Tafsīr*, 27:48, lines 3–4); *fuʾād* and *qalb* are synonyms.

7. Jorge Luis Borges, *El tintorero enmascarado Hâkim de Merv*, in *Obras completas* (Buenos Aires, 1974), 324–325.

8. W. Madelung and P. E. Walker, *An Ismaili Heresiography: The "Bâb al-shaytân" from Abû Tammâm's Kitâb al-shajara* (Leiden, 1998), 76–77 (Arabic text), 75 (translation). On this text, see also P. Walker, *An Ismaʿili Version of the Heresiography of the Seventy-two Erring Sects*, in *Medieval Ismaʿili History and Thought*, ed. F. Daftary (Cambridge, 1996), 161–162.

9. Al-Suyūtī, *Al-Laʾālī al-masnūʿa fī l-ahādīth al-mawdūʿa*, 2 vols. (Cairo, n.d.), 1:63–81; compare *TG*, 2:509.

10. Al-Tabarī, *Jāmiʿ al-bayān ʿan taʾwīl āy al-Qurʾān*, 27:48, 18–19 and before.

11. Al-Tabarī, *Taʾrīkh*, 1:1192, lines 3–4.; al-Tabarī, *Jāmiʿ al-bayān*, 17:186–187, but related to sura 22:52 and not to the passages in surat al-Najm.

12. See C. Gilliot in *Arabica* 32 (1985): 62–63.

13. *TG,* 2:452–453.

14. Regarding that attribution, however, see the remark by C. Gilliot in *Israel Oriental Studies* 19 (1999): 67–68.

15. See *TG,* 1:317, 4:393–394, and 1027 (index).

3. Theology and Science

1. As a general reference for this chapter, see *TG,* 4:459–477.

2. David Furley, in *Proceedings of the Boston Area Colloquium in Ancient Philosophy,* vol. 2, ed. J.-J. Cleary (Lanham, 1986), 1–2.

3. *TG,* 2:499–500, 454–455.

4. Ibid., 442–449, 450–452, 495, 500.

5. I am thinking of the famous "Theology of Aristotle," but also of other texts such as the later *Liber de Causis;* see F. Zimmermann in *Pseudo-Aristotle in the Middle Ages,* ed. Jill Kraye et al. (London, 1986), 110–111.

6. *TG,* 3:37–44.

7. Ibid., 224–225; compare 67–70.

8. Ibid., 229–230, 280–282.

9. Ibid., 231–232, 4:446–447.

10. At the time, the pre-Socratics were recast as Neoplatonists in an apocryphal text attributed to Ammonius Saccas; see U. Rudolph, *Die Doxographie des Pseudo-Ammonios: Ein Beitrag zur neoplatonischen Überlieferung im Islam* (Stuttgart, 1989).

11. *TG,* 1:418–443.
12. Ibid., 2:398–400.
13. Ibid., 1:442.
14. Ibid., 3:233–234, 314–316.
15. Ibid., 234–235.
16. Ibid., 255–263.
17. For that later phase, see A. Dhanani, *The Physical Theory of Kalâm: Atoms, Space, and Void in Basrian Muʿtazilî Cosmology* (Leiden, 1994).
18. *TG,* 3:331–352.
19. Ibid., 309–323.
20. Ibid., 309.
21. Ibid., 6:19–20 (n. 33).
22. Ibid., 3:316–317.
23. Ibid., 67.
24. Ibid., 225–227.
25. Ibid., 227; see the diagram in Dhanani, *Physical Theory of Kalâm,* 135.
26. Schlomo Pines, *Beiträge zur islamischen Atomenlehre* (Berlin, 1936).
27. *TG,* 3:241–243.
28. Ibid., 233–236.
29. Ibid., 236, 121 (with correction 5:307).
30. Ibid., 4:473–474, 479.
31. Ibid., 6:23n38, 3:319.
32. Ibid., 6:21–22, 22n36.
33. Ibid., 3:320, 323–324.

34. Ibid., 236–237.
35. Dhanani, *Physical Theory of Kalâm,* 177–180.
36. *TG,* 4:4–5, 467–468.
37. Ibid., 137–138.
38. Ibid., 3:425–426.
39. Compare ibid., 4:479–480 and 513–517, plus the references indicated there.
40. Ibid., 3:367–369.
41. Ibid., 317.
42. Ibid., 428–445.
43. Ibid., 4:468–470.
44. Ibid., 476–477, 558.
45. F. Meier, *Bahâ'-i Walad: Grundzüge seines Lebens und seiner Mystik* (Leiden, 1989), 436–439.

4. Theology and Human Reality

1. Here I am summarizing *TG,* 4:695–717.
2. At least for the theologians: the writings composed by the *kuttāb* ('Abd al-Hamīd b. Yahyā, Ibn al-Muqaffa', and so on) and the mirrors of princes had a happier fate.
3. *TG,* 1:169–171, 175–176.
4. Ibid., 183–184.
5. Ibid., 2:271–273.
6. Or to use Arabic terminology, with the condemnation of *sabb al-sahāba,* polemicizing against the Companions: see *TG,* 1:236–237, 2:436, 3:451.

7. See E. Landau-Tasseron in *Der Islam* 67 (1990): 2–3.

8. *TG*, 4:14–15.

9. Ibid., 3:439.

10. Ibid., 4:700.

11. Ibid., 3:129–130.

12. Ibid., 1:308–312.

13. Ibid., 2:387–391.

14. Ibid., 4:703–706.

15. Ibid., 1:87, 2:493. Jahm was a follower of Hārith b. Surayj, who had risen up against the Umayyad regime with the watchword *irjāʾ*.

16. Ibid., 408–409.

17. Ibid., 1:86–88.

18. Ibid., 4:709–710.

19. Ibid., 3:55–57.

20. Ibid., 55.

21. Ibid., 4:711.

22. Ibid., 3:109–112.

23. Ibid., 173–175.

24. Ibid., 416.

25. Ibid., 2:408–409, 4:714–715.

26. Ibid., 2:388, 3:174, 199–200.

27. Ibid., 4:46.

28. Ibid., 3:130–133, 4:88–94.

29. Ibid., 4:716.

30. Ibid., 69–70.

31. For them, see A. T. Karamustafa, *God's Unruly Friends* (Salt Lake City, 1994).

5. Theology and Its Principles

1. See G. Söhngen in *Lexikon für Theologie und Kirche,* 11 vols. (Freiburg, 1957–1967), 3:89. A theological evaluation is given in H. Schütze-Eichel, "Credo quia absurdum est?" *Trierer Theologische Zeitschrift* 84 (1975): 156ff.

2. *TG* 4:205–206, 198.

3. Ibid., 92–93, 295–296; see also my "Skepticism in Islamic Thought," *Al-Abhāth* 21 (1968): 1ff.

4. From 'Askar Mukram, where there were many Mu'tazilites.

5. A German translation and commentary appear in *TG,* 5:161–162.

6. Ibid., 1:34–35.

7. See quotation, ibid., 5:163.

8. Ibid., 3:292–293.

9. Up to now, there has been a tendency to read Shāfi'ī through the eyes of later theoreticians of his school, who projected their quadripartite schema onto his *Risāla* (Epistle). But J. E. Lowry, "Legal-Theoretical Content of the *Risala* of Muhammad b. Idris al-Shafi'i" (Ph.D. diss., University of Pennsylvania, 1999), has clearly shown that the concept of *bayān* dominating Shāfi'ī's thought turns essentially on correspondences between the Koran and the sunna. For the *ijmā',* see 43ff. and 426ff.

10. For Wāsil, see *TG,* 2:279–280 and 4:649–650.

11. For Al-Jubbā'i, see D. Gimaret, *Une lecture mu'tazilite du Coran: Le Tafsīr d'Abū 'Alī al-Djubbā'ī (m. 303/915) partiellement reconstitué à partir de ses citateurs* (Louvain, 1994). For Abū 'l-Qasīm al-Balkhī (d. AH 319/931 CE), see *Encyclopaedia Iranica,* ed. Ehsan Yarshater (London, 1985–), 1:360b, s.v. "Abū 'l-Qāsem al-Ka'bī." For Abū Muslim al-Isfahānī (d. AH 322/934 CE), see *TG,* 1:430–431. For al-Asamm, see 2:403–404, and for 'Amr b. 'Ubayd, 298–299.

12. Suras 25:33 and 3:7.

13. Daniel 2:7 and 5:12. When in Arabic the verb appears in its second form *(fassara),* this is also Syriac (Brockelmann, *Lexicon Syriacum,* 615a).

14. See *TG,* 4:984, index of terms.

15. Ibid., 3:51–52, 384; see the text I published in *Der Orient in der Forschung: Festschrift O. Spies,* ed. W. Hoenerbach (Wiesbaden, 1967), 170ff.

16. Sura 8:65.

17. *TG,* 3:266–267, 4:650–651; see in general, and also for what follows, my "L'autorité de la tradition prophétique dans la théologie mu'tazilite," in *La notion d'autorité au Moyen Âge: Islam, Byzance, Occident* (Paris, 1982), 211ff.

18. *TG* 3:60, 4:652.

19. Shāfi'ī, *Al-Risāla,* ed. Ahmad Muhammad Shākir (Cairo, AH 1358/1940 CE), 169ff., §§998–1308; compare Lowry, *Legal-Theoretical Content,* 261ff.

20. *TG,* 3:383.

21. Ibid., 4:113–114.

22. Ibid., 3:306.

23. Ibid., 410–411.

24. Ibid., 4:42–43.

25. See my *Die Erkenntnislehre des 'Adudaddīn al-Īcī* (Wiesbaden, 1966), 400.

26. *TG*, 2:133–134.

27. Ibid., 4:654.

28. Lowry, *Legal-Theoretical Content*, 427ff.

29. *TG*, 4:655.

30. Ibid., 3:51.

31. Ibid., 4:657.

32. 'Abd al-Qāhir al-Baghdādī, *Usūl al-Dīn* (Istanbul, 1928), 19, lines 6–7.

33. *TG*, 3:385–386.

34. Lowry, *Legal-Theoretical Content*, 436.

35. *TG*, 3:384, 4:656–657.

36. See, for example, his opinion on the *tafra*, ibid., 4:419; for the description of Al-Nazzām's character, see 3:306.

37. Ibid., 4:657.

38. Ibid., 3:390–391.

39. For Iyās b. Mu'āwiya, see ibid., 2:154–155. For Sha'bi, see G. H. A. Juynboll entry, *Encyclopaedia of Islam*, 2d ed., (Leiden, 1960–2004), 9:162–163.

40. *TG*, 2:191, 143–144.

41. Ibid., 4:664.

42. Shāfi'ī would later use the term *ma'nā* instead of

'illa—see W. Hallaq in *Der Islam* 64 (1987): 45—but that does not necessarily mean that elsewhere *'illa* was not already in use. Shāfiʿī was never influenced by Basrian thought. Lowry, *Legal-Theoretical Content*, translates *ma'nā* as "policy reason" (211–212).

43. *Al-Risāla ilā 'Uthmān al-Battī*, ed. Muhammad Zāhid al-Kawtharī, with the *Kitāb al-'ālim wal-muta'allim* (Cairo, 1368/1949), 34ff.; compare *TG*, 1:192ff.

44. Compare the two texts in *TG*, 5:171–172, nn. 5–6; see also 2:302, 4:662. In grammar, the search for the *'illa*, the cause of the evolution of language and its irregularities, remained characteristic of the Basrian "school."

45. Ibid., 2:161–162; see also my "La liberté du juge dans le milieu basrien du VIIIe siècle," in *La notion de liberté au Moyen Âge*, 25ff.

46. See the texts mentioned in *TG*, 5:118–119.

47. The *mazālim* courts are different; see *Encyclopaedia of Islam*, 2d ed., 6:933–934.

48. Lowry, *Legal-Theoretical Content*, 359. The essential point is that in Islam everyone must apply the law in his or her own ritual duties.

49. *TG*, 3:176ff.

50. See, for Bishr, ibid., 187; for al-Asamm, ibid., 2:415–416; see also the summary in 4:662–663, where their position is compared with Shāfiʿī's.

51. Ibid., 3:387.

52. Ibid., 6:190, text 255c. The case of the *ibn al-sabīl* was

also discussed by Shāfiʿī, *Risāla* §352; compare Lowry, *Legal-Theoretical Content*, 450.

53. That attitude would be propagated openly only two generations later, by Dāwūd b. ʿAlī al-Isbahānī (d. AH 270/884 CE). He was often in contact with the Muʿtazilites (see *TG*, 4:223–224); he also studied with Abū ʿAbd al-Rahmān al-Shāfiʿī, the disciple of Abū ʾl-Hudhayl, but Dāwūd's father was a Hanafite.

54. On this term, see my article in *Encyclopaedia of Islam*, 2d ed., 10:341–342, s.v. "Tashbīh wa-tanzīh."

55. The only possible exception is the *ijmāʿ*. Schacht has noted its affinity to the *opinio prudentium* of Roman law. Greek philosophers spoke of *koinōnia tōn anthrōpōn*. But the resemblances are deceptive, and direct influence is impossible to prove (see *TG*, 4:655). The equivalent of *qiyas al-ghāʾib ʿalā ʾl-shāhid* is *analogismos*, which in the Arabic version of Galen of Pergamum's *Peri tes iatrikes empeirias* was translated as *qiyās bi-ʾl-zāhir ʿalā ʾl-khafī* (see *TG*, 4:665). On the question whether the influence of the Stoic *sēmeion, sēmeiōton, sēmeiōsis* can be seen in the nomenclature *dalīl, madlūl, istidlāl*, see my "The Logical Structure of Islamic Theology," in *Logic in Classical Islamic Culture*, ed. G. E. von Grunebaum (Wiesbaden, 1970), 21–22.

56. *TG*, 3:45–46, 4:502–503.

57. The first was probably Bishr b. al-Muʿtamir (ibid., 5:231, "Widerlegungen," B1); Abū ʾl-Hudhayl espe-

cially attacked Hafs al-Fard, who was Dirār's most eminent disciple (ibid., 2:729–730, 3:48, 276).

58. Bishr b. al-Muʿtamir did the same, but the antonym he used was not *darūrī* but *ibtidāʾī*, "given in advance" (ibid., 3:118).

59. *Masʾūliyya* is a recent term: R. Dozy, *Supplément aux dictionnaires arabes,* 1:621b, recognizes the word only through Butrus al-Bustānī's *Muhīt al-Muhīt,* with the meaning "obligation"—despite the fact that *masʾūl* is Koranic.

60. *TG,* 3:252–353.

61. Ibid., 4:361–362.

62. Ibid., 3:231–232.

63. Ibid., 168–169, 4:99–100.

64. See my *Die Erkenntnislehre,* 329–330; see also my "Early Islamic Theologians on the Existence of God," in *Islam and the Medieval West,* ed. K. I. Semaan (New York, 1980), 64ff.

65. Published by M. Meyerhof and J. Schacht under the title *The Theologus Autodidactus of Ibn al-Nafis* (Oxford, 1968).

66. *TG,* 4:669–670.

67. See, for Bishr b. al-Muʿtamir, ibid., 3:109–110.

68. Ibid., 138–139.

69. For this term, see D. Gimaret, *La doctrine d'al-Ashʿarī* (Paris, 1990), 470n2.

70. *TG,* 4:671.

71. This was not purely imaginary. Rather, he tells of

episodes in a middle-class salon in Basra, where al-
Nazzām had taken the side of the dog while a
Mu'tazilite colleague had defended the cock.

72. *TG*, 4:727–728.
73. Ibid., 3:254. According to him, that was especially
true of sense perceptions. Later, the universal laws
of thought, such as the principle of the excluded
third term, were added. These laws exist in us a priori (see my *Die Erkenntnislehre*, 164ff.). The sequence
zann—i'tiqād—'ilm by which knowledge advances toward certainty is reminiscent of the Kantian hierar-
chy *Meinen—Glauben—Wissen* (*Kritik der reinen
Vernunft*, B 850—Transzendentale Methodenlehre,
2:3).
74. *TG*, 3:380.
75. Ibid., 4:102–103.
76. Ibid., 97–98.
77. Sura 63:1.
78. See *Wörterbuch der klassischen arabischen Sprache*,
1:90a, 91b.
79. *TG*, 4:128.
80. See, for the details of the discussion, ibid., 320ff.
81. See my "Göttliche Allmacht im Zerrbild
menschlicher Sprache," *Mélanges de l'Université Saint-
Joseph* 49 (1975–1976): 653ff.

INDEX